I0167220

Mohammedanism
Lectures on Its Origin, Its Religious and Political Growth, and Its Present State

C. Snouck Hurgronje

Contents

MOHAMMEDANISM
LECTURES ON ITS ORIGIN, ITS RELIGIOUS AND POLITICAL GROWTH, AND ITS PRESENT STATE

by

C. Snouck Hurgronje

AMERICAN LECTURES ON THE HISTORY OF RELIGIONS

SERIES OF 1914-1915

1916

ANNOUNCEMENT

THE American Lectures on the History of Religions are delivered under the auspices of the American Committee for Lectures on the History of Religions. This Committee was organized in 1892, for the purpose of instituting "popular courses in the History of Religions, somewhat after the style of the Hibbert Lectures in England, to be delivered by the best scholars of Europe and this country, in various cities, such as Baltimore, Boston, Brooklyn, Chicago, New York, Philadelphia."

The terms of association under which the Committee exists are as follows:

1. — The object of this Committee shall be to provide courses of lectures on the history of religions, to be delivered in various cities.

2. — The Committee shall be composed of delegates from the institutions agreeing to co-operate, with such additional members as may be chosen by these delegates.

3. — These delegates — one from each institution, with the additional members selected — shall constitute themselves a council under the name of the "American Committee for Lectures on the History of Religions."

4. — The Committee shall elect out of its number a Chairman, a Secretary, and a Treasurer.

5. — All matters of local detail shall be left to the co-operating institutions under whose auspices the lectures are to be delivered.

6. — A course of lectures on some religion, or phase of religion, from an historical point of view, or on a subject germane to the study of religions, shall be delivered annually, or at such intervals as may be found practicable, in the different cities represented by this Committee.

7.—The Committee (a) shall be charged with the selection of the lectures, (b) shall have charge of the funds, (c) shall assign the time for the lectures in each city, and perform such other functions as may be necessary.

8.—Polemical subjects, as well as polemics in the treatment of subjects, shall be positively excluded.

9.—The lectures shall be delivered in the various cities between the months of September and June.

10.—The copyright of the lectures shall be the property of the Committee.

11.—The compensation of the lecturer shall be fixed in each case by the Committee.

12.—The lecturer shall be paid in installments after each course, until he shall have received half of the entire compensation. Of the remaining half, one half shall be paid to him upon delivery of the manuscript, properly prepared for the press, and the second half on the publication of the volume, less a deduction for corrections made by the author in the proofs.

The Committee as now constituted is as follows: Prof. Crawford H. Toy, Chairman, 7 Lowell St., Cambridge, Mass.; Rev. Dr. John P. Peters, Treasurer, 227 W. 99th St., New York City; Prof. Morris Jastrow, Jr., Secretary, 248 So. 23d St., Philadelphia, Pa.; President Francis Brown, Union Theological Seminary, New York City; Prof. Richard Gottheil, Columbia University, New York City; Prof. Harry Pratt Judson, University of Chicago, Chicago, Ill.; Prof. Paul Haupt, Johns Hopkins University, Baltimore, Md.; Mr. Charles D. Atkins, Director, Brooklyn Institute of Arts and Sciences; Prof. E.W. Hopkins, Yale University, New Haven, Conn.; Prof. Edward Knox Mitchell, Hartford Theological Seminary, Hartford, Conn.; President F.K. Sanders, Washburn College, Topeka, Kan.; Prof. H.P. Smith, Meadville Theological Seminary, Meadville, Pa.; Prof. W.J. Hinke, Auburn Theological Seminary, Auburn, N.Y.; Prof. Kemper Fullerton, Oberlin Theological Seminary, Oberlin, N.Y.

The lecturers in the course of American Lectures on the History of Religions and the titles of their volumes are as follows:

1894-1895—Prof. T.W. Rhys-Davids, Ph.D.,— *Buddhism*.

1896-1897—Prof. Daniel G. Brinton, M.D., LL.D.— *Religions of Primitive Peoples*.

1897-1898—Rev. Prof. T.K. Cheyne, D.D.—*Jewish Religious Life after the Exile*.

1898-1899—Prof. Karl Budde, D.D.—*Religion of Israel to the Exile*.

1904-1905—Prof. George Steindorff, Ph.D.—*The Religion of the Ancient Egyptians*.

1905-1906—Prof. George W. Knox, D.D., LL.D.—*The Development of Religion in Japan*.

1906-1907—Prof. Maurice Bloomfield, Ph.D., LL.D.—*The Religion of the Veda*.

1907-1908—Prof. A.V.W. Jackson, Ph.D., LL.D.—*The Religion of Persia*.[1]

1909-1910—Prof. Morris Jastrow, Jr., Ph.D.—*Aspects of Religious Belief and Practice in Babylonia and Assyria*.

1910-1911—Prof. J.J.M. DeGroot—*The Development of Religion in China*.

1911-1912—Prof. Franz Cumont.[2]—*Astrology and Religion among the Greeks and Romans*.

The lecturer for 1914 was Professor C. Snouck Hurgronje. Born in Oosterhout, Holland, in 1857, he studied Theology and Oriental Languages at the University of Leiden and continued his studies at the University of Strassburg. In 1880 he published his first important work *Het Mekkaansch Feest*, having resolved to devote himself entirely to the study of Mohammedanism in its widest aspects. After a few years' activity as Lecturer on Mohammedan Law at the Seminary for Netherlands-India in Leiden, he spent eight months (1884-5) in Mecca and Jidda. In 1888, he became lecturer at the University of Leiden and in the same year was sent out as Professor to Batavia in Netherlands-India, where he spent the years 1889-1906. Upon his return he was appointed Professor of Arabic at the University of Leiden. Among his principal published works may be mentioned: *Mekka*, The Hague, 1888-9;

---

1 This course was not published by the Committee, but will form part of Prof. Jackson's volume on the Religion of Persia in the series of *Handbooks on the History of Religions*, edited by Prof. Morris Jastrow, Jr., and published by Messrs. Ginn & Company of Boston. Prof. Jastrow's volume is, therefore, the eighth in the series.

2 Owing to special circumstances, Prof. Cumont's volume was published before that of Prof. DeGroot. It is, therefore, the ninth in the series and that of Prof. DeGroot the tenth.

De Beteekenis van den Islam voor zijne Belijders in Oost Indie, Leiden, 1883; *Mekkanische Sprichwoerter*, The Hague, 1886; *De Atjehers*, Leiden, 1903-4, England tr. London, 1906; *Het Gajoland en zijne Bezvoners*, Batavia, 1903, and *Nederland en de Islam*, Leiden, 1915.

The lectures to be found in the present volume were delivered before the following Institutions: Columbia University, Yale University, The University of Pennsylvania, Meadville Theological Seminary, The University of Chicago, The Lowell Institute, and the Johns Hopkins University.

The Committee owes a debt of deep gratitude to Mr. Charles R. Crane for having made possible the course of lectures for the year 1914.

RICHARD GOTTHEIL
CRAWFORD H. TOY
Committee on Publication.
April, 1916.

Mohammedanism

I

Some Points Concerning The Origin Of Islam

THERE are more than two hundred million people who call themselves after the name of Mohammed, would not relinquish that name at any price, and cannot imagine a greater blessing for the remainder of humanity than to be incorporated into their communion. Their ideal is no less than that the whole earth should join in the faith that there is no god but Allah and that Mohammed is Allah's last and most perfect messenger, who brought the latest and final revelation of Allah to humanity in Allah's own words. This alone is enough to claim our special interest for the Prophet, who in the seventh century stirred all Arabia into agitation and whose followers soon after his death founded an empire extending from Morocco to China.

Even those who—to my mind, not without gross exaggeration—would seek the explanation of the mighty stream of humanity poured out by the Arabian peninsula since 630 over Western and Middle Asia, Northern Africa, and Southern Europe principally in geographic and economic causes, do not ignore the fact that it was Mohammed who opened the sluice gates. It would indeed be difficult to maintain that without his preaching the Arabs of the seventh century would have been induced by circumstances to swallow up the empire of the Sasanids and to rob the Byzantine Empire of some of its richest provinces. However great a weight one may give to political and economic factors, it was religion, Islam, which in a certain sense united the hitherto hopelessly divided Arabs, Islam which enabled them to found an enormous international community; it was Islam which bound the speedily converted nations together even after the shattering of its political power, and which still binds them today when only a miserable remnant of that power remains.

The aggressive manner in which young Islam immediately put itself in opposition to the rest of the world had the natural consequence of awakening an interest which was far from being of a friendly nature. Moreover men were still very far from such a striving towards universal peace as would have induced a patient study of the means of bringing the different peoples into close spiritual relationship, and therefore from an endeavour to understand the spiritual life of races different to their own. The Christianity of that time was itself by no means averse to the forcible extension of its faith, and in the community of Mohammedans which systematically attempted to reduce the world to its authority by force of arms, it saw only an enemy whose annihilation was, to its regret, beyond its power. Such an enemy it could no more observe impartially than one modern nation can another upon which it considers it necessary to make war. Everything maintained or invented to the disadvantage of Islam was greedily absorbed by Europe; the picture which our forefathers in the Middle Ages formed of Mohammed's religion appears to us a malignant caricature. The rare theologians[3] who, before attacking the false faith, tried to form a clear notion of it, were not listened to, and their merits have only become appreciated in our own time. A vigorous combating of the prevalent fictions concerning Islam would have exposed a scholar to a similar treatment to that which, fifteen years ago, fell to the lot of any Englishman who maintained the cause of the Boers; he would have been as much of an outcast as a modern inhabitant of Mecca who tried to convince his compatriots of the virtues of European policy and social order.

Two and a half centuries ago, a prominent Orientalist[4], who wrote an exposition of Mohammed's teaching, felt himself obliged to give an elaborate justification

---

3   See for instance the reference to the exposition of the Paderborn bishop Olivers (1227) in the Paderborn review *Theologie und Glaube*, Jahrg. iv., p. 535, etc. (*Islam*, iv., p. 186); also some of the accounts mentioned in Gueterbock, *Der Islam im Lichte der byzantinischen Polemik*, etc.

4   J.H. Hottinger, *Historia Orientalis*, Zuerich, 1651 (2d. edition 1660).

of his undertaking in his "Dedicatio." He appeals to one or two celebrated predecessors and to learned colleagues, who have expressly instigated him to this work.
Amongst other things he quotes a letter from the Leiden professor, L'Empereur,
in which he conjures Breitinger by the bowels of Jesus Christ ("per viscera Jesu
Christi") to give the young man every opportunity to complete his study of the
religion of Mohammed, "which so far has only been treated in a senseless way."
As a fruit of this study L'Empereur thinks it necessary to mention in the first place
the better understanding of the (Christian) Holy Scriptures by the extension of our
knowledge of Oriental manners and customs. Besides such promotion of Christian
exegesis and apologetics and the improvement of the works on general history,
Hottinger himself contemplated a double purpose in his *Historia Orientalis*. The
Roman Catholics often vilified Protestantism by comparing the Reformed doctrine
to that of Mohammedanism; this reproach of Crypto-mohammedanism Hottinger
wished "talionis lege" to fling back at the Catholics; and he devotes a whole chapter
(Cap. 6) of his book to the demonstration that Bellarminius' proofs of the truth of
the Church doctrine might have been copied from the Moslim dogma. In the second place, conforming to the spirit of the times, he wished, just as Bibliander had
done in his refutation of the Qoran, to combine the combat against Mohammedan
unbelief with that against the Turkish Empire ("in oppugnationem Mahometanae
perfidiae et Turcici regni").

The Turks were feared by the Europe of that time, and the significance of their
religion for their worldly power was well known; thus the political side of the
question gave Hottinger's work a special claim to consideration. Yet, in spite of all
this, Hottinger feared that his labour would be regarded as useless, or even wicked.
Especially when he is obliged to say anything favourable of Mohammed and his
followers, he thinks it necessary to protect himself against misconstruction by the
addition of some selected terms of abuse. When mentioning Mohammed's name, he
says: "at the mention of whom the mind shudders" ("ad cujus profecto mentionem
inhorrescere nobis debet animus"). The learned Abbe Maracci, who in 1698 pro-
duced a Latin translation of the Qoran accompanied by an elaborate refutation, was
no less than Hottinger imbued with the necessity of shuddering at every mention of
the "false" Prophet, and Dr. Prideaux, whose *Vie de Mahomet* appeared in the same
year in Amsterdam, abused and shuddered with them, and held up his biography of

Mohammed as a mirror to "unbelievers, atheists, deists, and libertines."

It was a Dutch scholar, H. Reland, the Utrecht professor of theology, who in the beginning of the eighteenth century frankly and warmly recommended the application of historical justice even towards the Mohammedan religion; in his short Latin sketch of Islam[5] he allowed the Mohammedan authorities to speak for themselves. In his "Dedicatio" to his brother and in his extensive preface he explains his then new method. Is it to be supposed, he asks, that a religion as ridiculous as the Islam described by Christian authors should have found millions of devotees? Let the Moslims themselves describe their own religion for us; just as the Jewish and Christian religions are falsely represented by the heathen and Protestantism by Catholics, so every religion is misrepresented by its antagonists. "We are mortals, subject to error; especially where religious matters are concerned, we often allow ourselves to be grossly misled by passion." Although it may cause evil-minded readers to doubt the writer's orthodoxy he continues to maintain that truth can only be served by combating her opponents in an honourable way.

"No religion," says Reland, "has been more calumniated than Islam," although the Abbe Maracci himself could give no better explanation of the turning of many Jews and Christians to this religion than the fact that it contains many elements of natural truth, evidently borrowed from the Christian religion, "which seem to be in accordance with the law and the light of nature" ("quae naturae legi ac lumini consentanea videntur"). "More will be gained for Christianity by friendly intercourse with Mohammedans than by slander; above all Christians who live in the East must not, as is too often the case, give cause to one Turk to say to another who suspects him of lying or deceit: 'Do you take me for a Christian?' ("putasne me Christianum esse"). In truth, the Mohammedans often put us to shame by their virtues; and a better knowledge of Islam can only help to make our irrational pride give place to gratitude to God for the undeserved mercy which He bestowed upon us in Christianity." Reland has no illusions that his scientific justice will find acceptance in a wide circle "as he becomes daily more and more convinced that the world wishes to be deceived and is governed by prejudice" ("qui quotidie magis magisque experior mundum decipi velle et praeconceptis opinionibus regi").

It was not long before the scale was turned in the opposite direction, and Islam

---

5   H. Relandi de religione Mohammedica libri duo, Utrecht, 1704 (2d ed. 1717).

was made by some people the object of panegyrics as devoid of scientific foundation as the former calumnies. In 1730 appeared in London the incomplete posthumous work of Count de Boulainvilliers, Vie de Mahomet, in which, amongst other things, he says of the Arabian Prophet that "all that he has said concerning the essential religious dogmas is true, but he has not said all that is true, and it is only therein that his religion differs from ours." De Boulainvilliers tells us with particular satisfaction that Mohammed, who respected the devotion of hermits and monks, proceeded with the utmost severity against the official clergy, condemning its members either to death or to the abjuration of their faith. This *Vie de Mahomet* was as a matter of fact an anti-clerical romance, the material of which was supplied by a superficial knowledge of Islam drawn from secondary sources. That a work with such a tendency was sure to arouse interest at that time, is shown by a letter from the publisher, Coderc, to Professor Gagnier at Oxford, in which he writes: "He [de Boulainvilliers] mixes up his history with many political reflections, which by their newness and boldness are sure to be well received" ("Il mele son Histoire de plusieurs reflexions politiques, et qui par leur hardiesse ne manqueront pas d'etre tres bien recues").

Jean Gagnier however considered these bold novelties very dangerous and endeavoured to combat them in another *Vie de Mahomet*, which appeared from his hand in 1748 at Amsterdam. He strives after a "juste milieu" between the too violent partisanship of Maracci and Prideaux and the ridiculous acclamations of de Boulainvilliers. Yet this does not prevent him in his preface from calling Mohammed the greatest villain of mankind and the most mortal enemy of God ("le plus scelerat de tous les hommes et le plus mortel ennemi de Dieu"). His desire to make his contemporaries proof against the poison of de Boulainvilliers' dangerous book gains the mastery over the pure love of truth for which Reland had so bravely striven.

Although Sale in his "Preliminary Discourse" to his translation of the Qoran endeavours to contribute to a fair estimation of Mohammed and his work, of which his motto borrowed from Augustine, "There is no false doctrine that does not contain some truth" ("nulla falsa doctrina est quae non aliquid veri permisceat"), is proof, still the prejudicial view remained for a considerable time the prevalent one. Mohammed was branded as *imposteur* even in circles where Christian fanaticism was out of the question. Voltaire did not write his tragedy *Mahomet ou le fanatisme* as a historical study; he was aware that his fiction was in many respects at variance with history. In writing his work he was, as he himself expresses it, inspired by "l'amour du genre humain et l'horreur du fanatisme." He wanted to put before the public an armed Tartufe and thought he might lay the part upon Mohammed, for, says he, "is not the man, who makes war against his own country and dares to do it in the name of God, capable of any ill?" The dislike that Voltaire had conceived for the Qoran from a superficial acquaintance with it, "ce livre inintelligible qui fait fremir le sens commun a chaque page," probably increased his unfavourable opinion, but the principal motive of his choice of a representative must have been that the general public still regarded Mohammed as the incarnation of fanaticism and priestcraft.

Almost a century lies between Gagnier's biography of Mohammed and that of the Heidelberg professor Weil (Mohammed der Prophet, sein Leben and seine Lehre, Stuttgart, 1843); and yet Weil did well to call Gagnier his last independent predecessor. Weil's great merit is, that he is the first in his field who instituted an extensive historico-critical investigation without any preconceived opinion. His final opinion of Mohammed is, with the necessary reservations: "In so far as he brought the most beautiful teachings of the Old and the New Testament to a people which was not illuminated by one ray of faith, he may be regarded, even by those who are not Mohammedans, as a messenger of God." Four years later Caussin de Perceval in his Essai sur l'histoire des Arabes, written quite independently of Weil, expresses the same idea in these words: "It would be an injustice to Mohammed to consider him as no more than a clever impostor, an ambitious man of genius; he was in the first place a man convinced of his vocation to deliver his nation from error and to regenerate it."

About twenty years later the biography of Mohammed made an enormous advance through the works of Muir, Sprenger, and Noldeke. On the ground of much wider and at the same time deeper study of the sources than had been possible for Weil and Caussin de Perceval, each of these three scholars gave in his own way an account of the origin of Islam. Noldeke was much sharper and more cautious in his historical criticism than Muir or Sprenger. While the biographies written by these two men have now only historical value, Noldeke's *History of the Qoran* is still an indispensable instrument of study more than half a century after its first appearance. Numbers of more or less successful efforts to make Mohammed's life understood by the nineteenth century intellect have followed these without much permanent gain. Mohammed, who was represented to the public in turn as deceiver, as a genius mislead by the Devil, as epileptic, as hysteric, and as prophet, was obliged later on even to submit to playing on the one hand the part of socialist and, on the other hand, that of a defender of capitalism. These points of view were principally characteristic of the temperament of the scholars who held them; they did not really advance our understanding of the events that took place at Mecca and Medina between 610 and 632 A.D., that prologue to a perplexing historical drama.

The principal source from which all biographers started and to which they always returned, was the Qoran, the collection of words of Allah spoken by Mohammed in those twenty-two years. Hardly anyone, amongst the "faithful" and the "unfaithful," doubts the generally authentic character of its contents except the Parisian professor Casanova[6]. He tried to prove a little while ago that Mohammed's revelations originally contained the announcement that the HOUR, the final catastrophe, the Last judgment would come during his life. When his death had therefore falsified this prophecy, according to Casanova, the leaders of the young community found themselves obliged to submit the revelations preserved in writing or memory to a thorough revision, to add some which announced the mortality even of the last prophet, and, finally to console the disappointed faithful with the hope of Mohammed's return before the end of the world. This doctrine of the return, mentioned neither in the Qoran nor in the eschatological tradition of later times, according to Casanova was afterwards changed again into the expectation of the Mahdi, the last of Mohammed's deputies, "a Guided of God," who shall be descended from Mohammed, bear his name, resemble him in appearance, and who shall fill the world once more before its end with justice, as it is now filled with injustice and tyranny.

In our sceptical times there is very little that is above criticism, and one day or other we may expect to hear that Mohammed never existed. The arguments for this

---

6 Paul Casanova, Mohammed et la fin du monde, Paris, 1911. His hypotheses are founded upon Weil's doubts of the authenticity of a few verses of the *Qoran* (iii., 138; xxxix., 31, etc.), which doubts were sufficiently refuted half a century ago by Noldeke in his *Geschichte des Qorans*, 1st edition, p. 197, etc.

can hardly be weaker than those of Casanova against the authenticity of the Qoran. Here we may acknowledge the great power of what has been believed in all times, in all places, by all the members of the community ("quod semper, quod ubique, quod ab omnibus creditum est"). For, after the death of Mohammed there immediately arose a division which none of the leading personalities were able to escape, and the opponents spared each other no possible kind of insult, scorn, or calumny. The enemies of the first leaders of the community could have wished for no more powerful weapon for their attack than a well-founded accusation of falsifying the word of God. Yet this accusation was never brought against the first collectors of the scattered revelations; the only reproach that was made against them in connexion with this labour being that verses in which the Holy Family (Ali and Fatimah) were mentioned with honour, and which, therefore, would have served to support the claims of the Alids to the succession of Mohammed, were suppressed by them. This was maintained by the Shi'ites, who are unsurpassed in Islam as falsifiers of history; and the passages which, according to them, are omitted from the official Qoran would involve precisely on account of their reference to the succession, the mortality of Mohammed. All sects and parties have the same text of the Qoran. This may have its errors and defects, but intentional alterations or mutilations of real importance are not to blame for this.

Now this rich authentic source — this collection of wild, poetic representations of the Day of judgment; of striving against idolatry; of stories from Sacred History; of exhortation to the practice of the cardinal virtues of the Old and New Testament; of precepts to reform the individual, domestic, and tribal life in the spirit of these virtues; of incantations and forms of prayer and a hundred things besides — is not always comprehensible to us. Even for the parts which we do understand, we are not able to make out the chronological arrangement which is necessary to gain an insight into Mohammed's personality and work. This is not only due to the form of the oracles, which purposely differs from the usual tone of mortals by its unctuousness and rhymed prose, but even more to the circumstance that all that the hearers could know, is assumed to be known. So the Qoran is full of references that are enigmatical to us. We therefore need additional explanation, and this can only be derived from tradition concerning the circumstances under which each revelation was delivered.

And, truly, the sacred tradition of Islam is not deficient in data of this sort. In the canonical and half-canonical collections of tradition concerning what the Prophet has said, done, and omitted to do, in biographical works, an answer is given to every question which may arise in the mind of the reader of the Qoran; and there are many Qoran-commentaries, in which these answers are appended to the verses which they are supposed to elucidate. Sometimes the explanations appear to us, even at first sight, improbable and unacceptable; sometimes they contradict each other; a good many seem quite reasonable.

The critical biographers of Mohammed have therefore begun their work of sifting by eliminating the improbable and by choosing between contradictory data by means of critical comparison. Here the gradually increasing knowledge of the spirit of the different parties in Islam was an important aid, as of course each group represented the facts in the way which best served their own purposes.

However cautiously and acutely Weil and his successors have proceeded, the continual progress of the analysis of the legislative as well as of the historical tradition of Islam since 1870 has necessitated a renewed investigation. In the first place it has become ever more evident that the thousands of traditions about Mohammed, which, together with the Qoran, form the foundation upon which the doctrine and life of the community are based, are for the most part the conventional expression of all the opinions which prevailed amongst his followers during the first three centuries after the Hijrah. The fiction originated a long time after Mohammed's death; during the turbulent period of the great conquests there was no leisure for such work. Our own conventional insincerities differ so much—externally at least—from those of that date, that it is difficult for us to realize a spiritual atmosphere where "pious fraud" was practised on such a scale. Yet this is literally true: in the first centuries of Islam no one could have dreamt of any other way of gaining acceptance for a doctrine or a precept than by circulating a tradition, according to which Mohammed had preached the doctrine or dictated it or had lived according to the precept. The whole individual, domestic, social, and political life as it developed in the three centuries during which the simple Arabian religion was adjusted to the complicated civilization of the great nations of that time, that all life was theoretically justified by representing it as the application of minute laws supposed to have been elaborated by Mohammed by precept and example.

Thus tradition gives invaluable material for the knowledge of the conflict of opinions in the first centuries, a strife the sharpness of which has been blunted in later times by a most resourceful harmonistic method. But, it is vain to endeavour to construct the life and teaching of Mohammed from such spurious accounts; they cannot even afford us a reliable illustration of his life in the form of "table talk," as an English scholar rather naively tried to derive from them. In a collection of this sort, supported by good external evidence, there would be attributed to the Prophet of Mecca sayings from the Old and New Testament, wise saws from classical and Arabian antiquity, prescriptions of Roman law and many other things, each text of which was as authentic as its fellows.

Anyone who, warned by Goldziher and others, has realized how matters stand in this respect, will be careful not to take the legislative tradition as a direct instrument for the explanation of the Qoran. When, after a most careful investigation of thousands of traditions which all appear equally old, we have selected the oldest, then we shall see that we have before us only witnesses of the first century of the Hijrah. The connecting threads with the time of Mohammed must be supplied for a great part by imagination.

The historical or biographical tradition in the proper sense of the word has only lately been submitted to a keener examination. It was known for a long time that here too, besides theological and legendary elements, there were traditions originating from party motive, intended to give an appearance of historical foundation to the particular interests of certain persons or families; but it was thought that after some sifting there yet remained enough to enable us to form a much clearer sketch of Mohammed's life than that of any other of the founders of a universal religion.

It is especially Prince Caetani and Father Lammens who have disturbed this illusion. According to them, even the data which had been pretty generally regarded as objective, rest chiefly upon tendentious fiction. The generations that worked at the biography of the Prophet were too far removed from his time to have true data or notions; and, moreover, it was not their aim to know the past as it was, but to construct a picture of it as it ought to have been according to their opinion. Upon the bare canvass of verses of the Qoran that need explanation, the traditionists have embroidered with great boldness scenes suitable to the desires or ideals of their particular group; or, to use a favourite metaphor of Lammens, they fill the empty spaces by a process of stereotyping which permits the critical observer to recognize the origin of each picture. In the Sirah (biography), the distance of the first describers from their object is the same as in the Hadith (legislative tradition); in both we get images of very distant things, perceived by means of fancy rather than by sight and taking different shapes according to the inclinations of each circle of describers.

Now, it may be true that the latest judges have here and there examined the Mohammedan traditions too sceptically and too suspiciously; nevertheless, it remains certain that in the light of their research, the method of examination cannot remain unchanged. We must endeavour to make our explanations of the Qoran independent of tradition, and in respect to portions where this is impossible, we must be suspicious of explanations, however apparently plausible.

During the last few years the accessible sources of information have considerably increased, the study of them has become much deeper and more methodical, and the result is that we can tell much less about the teaching and the life of Mohammed than could our predecessors half a century ago. This apparent loss is of course in reality nothing but gain.

Those who do not take part in new discoveries, nevertheless, wish to know now and then the results of the observations made with constantly improved instruments. Let me endeavour, very briefly, to satisfy this curiosity. That the report of the bookkeeping might make a somewhat different impression if another accountant had examined it, goes without saying, and sometimes I shall draw particular attention to my personal responsibility in this respect.

Of Mohammed's life before his appearance as the messenger of God, we know extremely little; compared to the legendary biography as treasured by the Faithful, practically nothing. Not to mention his pre-existence as a Light, which was with God, and for the sake of which God created the world, the Light, which as the principle of revelation, lived in all prophets from Adam onwards, and the final revelation of which in Mohammed was prophesied in the Scriptures of the Jews and the Christians; not to mention the wonderful and mysterious signs which announced the birth of the Seal of the Prophets, and many other features which the later Sirahs (biographies) and Maulids (pious histories of his birth, most in rhymed prose or in poetic metre) produce in imitation of the Gospels; even the elaborate discourses of the older biographies on occurrences, which in themselves might quite well come within the limits of sub-lunary possibility, do not belong to history. Fiction plays such a great part in these stories, that we are never sure of being on historical ground unless the Qoran gives us a firm footing.

The question, whether the family to which Mohammed belonged, was regarded as noble amongst the Qoraishites, the ruling tribe in Mecca, is answered in the affirmative by many; but by others this answer is questioned not without good grounds. The matter is not of prime importance, as there is no doubt that Mohammed grew up as a poor orphan and belonged to the needy and the neglected. Even a long time after his first appearance the unbelievers reproached him, according to the Qoran, with his insignificant worldly position, which fitted ill with a heavenly message; the same scornful reproach according to the Qoran was hurled at Mohammed's predecessors by sceptics of earlier generations; and it is well known that the stories of older times in the Qoran are principally reflections of what Mohammed himself experienced. The legends of Mohammed's relations to various members of his family are too closely connected with the pretensions of their descendants to have any value for biographic purposes. He married late an elderly woman, who, it is said, was able to lighten his material cares; she gave him the only daughter by whom he had descendants; descendants, who, from the Arabian point of view, do not count as such, as according to their genealogical theories the line of descent cannot pass through a woman. They have made an exception for the Prophet, as male offspring, the only blessing of marriage appreciated by Arabs, was withheld from him.

In the materialistic commercial town of Mecca, where lust of gain and usury reigned supreme, where women, wine, and gambling filled up the leisure time, where might was right, and widows, orphans, and the feeble were treated as superfluous ballast, an unfortunate being like Mohammed, if his constitution were sensitive, must have experienced most painful emotions. In the intellectual advantages that the place offered he could find no solace; the highly developed Arabian art of words, poetry with its fictitious amourettes, its polished descriptions of portions of Arabian nature, its venal vain praise and satire, might serve as dessert to a well-filled dish; they were unable to compensate for the lack of material prosperity. Mohammed felt his misery as a pain too great to be endured; in some way or other he must be delivered from it. He desired to be more than the greatest in his surroundings, and he knew that in that which they counted for happiness he could never even equal them. Rather than envy them regretfully, he preferred to despise their values of life, but on that very account he had to oppose these values with better ones.

It was not unknown in Mecca that elsewhere communities existed acquainted with such high ideals of life, spiritual goods accessible to the poor, even to them in particular. Apart from commerce, which brought the inhabitants of Mecca into contact with Abyssinians, Syrians, and others, there were far to the south and less far to the north and north-east of Mecca, Arabian tribes who had embraced the Jewish or the Christian religion. Perhaps this circumstance had helped to make the inhabitants of Mecca familiar with the idea of a creator, Allah, but this had little significance in their lives, as in the Maker of the Universe they did not see their Lawgiver and judge, but held themselves dependent for their good and evil fortune upon all manner of beings, which they rendered favourable or harmless by animistic practices. Thoroughly conservative, they did not take great interest in the conceptions of the "People of the Scripture," as they called the Jews, Christians, and perhaps some other sects arisen from these communities.

But Mohammed's deeply felt misery awakened his interest in them. Whether this had been the case with a few others before him in the milieu of Mecca, we need not consider, as it does not help to explain his actions. If wide circles had been anxious to know more about the contents of the "Scripture" Mohammed would not have felt in the dark in the way that he did. We shall probably never know, by intercourse with whom it really was that Mohammed at last gained some knowledge of the contents of the sacred books of Judaism and Christianity; probably through various people, and over a considerable length of time. It was not lettered men who satisfied his awakened curiosity; otherwise the quite confused ideas, especially in the beginning of the revelation, concerning the mutual relations between Jews and Christians could not be explained. Confusions between Miryam, the sister of Moses, and Mary, the mother of Jesus, between Saul and Gideon, mistakes about the relationship of Abraham to Isaac, Ishmael, and Jacob, might be put down to misconceptions of Mohammed himself, who could not all at once master the strange material. But his representation of Judaism and Christianity and a number of other forms of revelation, as almost identical in their contents, differing only in the place where, the time wherein, and the messenger of God by whom they came to man; this idea, which runs like a crimson thread through all the revelations of the first twelve years of Mohammed's prophecy, could not have existed if he had had an intimate acquaintance with Jewish or Christian men of letters. Moreover, the many post-biblical features and stories which the Qoran contains concerning the past of mankind, indicate a vulgar origin, and especially as regards the Christian legends, communications from people who lived outside the communion of the great Christian churches; this is sufficiently proved by the docetical representation of the death of Jesus and the many stories about his life, taken from apocryphal sources or from popular oral legends.

Mohammed's unlearned imagination worked all such material together into a religious history of mankind, in which Adam's descendants had become divided into innumerable groups of peoples differing in speech and place of abode, whose aim in life at one period or another came to resemble wonderfully that of the inhabitants of West- and Central-Arabia in the seventh century A.D. Hereby they strayed from the true path, in strife with the commands given by Allah. The whole of history, therefore, was for him a long series of repetitions of the antithesis between the foolishness of men, as this was now embodied in the social state of Mecca, and the wisdom of God, as known to the "People of the Scripture." To bring the erring ones back to the true path, it was Allah's plan to send them messengers from out of their midst, who delivered His ritual and His moral directions to them in His own words, who demanded the acknowledgment of Allah's omnipotence, and if they refused to follow the true guidance, threatened them with Allah's temporary or, even more, with His eternal punishment.

The antithesis is always the same, from Adam to Jesus, and the enumeration of the scenes is therefore rather monotonous; the only variety is in the detail, borrowed from biblical and apocryphal legends. In all the thousands of years the messengers of Allah play the same part as Mohammed finally saw himself called upon to play towards his people.

Mohammed's account of the past contains more elements of Jewish than of Christian origin, and he ignores the principal dogmas of the Christian Church. In spite of his supernatural birth, Jesus is only a prophet like Moses and others; and although his miracles surpass those of other messengers, Mohammed at a later period of his life is inclined to place Abraham above Jesus in certain respects. Yet the influence of Christianity upon Mohammed's vocation was very great; without the

Christian idea of the final scene of human history, of the Resurrection of the dead and the Last Judgment, Mohammed's mission would have no meaning. It is true, monotheism, in the Jewish sense, and after the contrast had become clear to Mohammed, accompanied by an express rejection of the Son of God and of the Trinity, has become one of the principal dogmas of Islam. But in Mohammed's first preaching, the announcement of the Day of judgment is much more prominent than the Unity of God; and it was against his revelations concerning Doomsday that his opponents directed their satire during the first twelve years. It was not love of their half-dead gods but anger at the wretch who was never tired of telling them, in the name of Allah, that all their life was idle and despicable, that in the other world they would be the outcasts, which opened the floodgates of irony and scorn against Mohammed. And it was Mohammed's anxiety for his own lot and that of those who were dear to him in that future life, that forced him to seek a solution of the question: who shall bring my people out of the darkness of antithesis into the light of obedience to Allah?

We should, *a posteriori*, be inclined to imagine a simpler answer to the question than that which Mohammed found; he might have become a missionary of Judaism or of Christianity to the Meccans. However natural such a conclusion may appear to us, from the premises with which we are acquainted, it did not occur to Mohammed. He began—the Qoran tells us expressly—by regarding the Arabs, or at all events *his* Arabs, as heretofore destitute of divine message[7]: "to whom We have sent no warner before you." Moses and Jesus—not to mention any others—had not been sent for the Arabs; and as Allah would not leave any section of mankind without a revelation, their prophet must still be to come. Apparently Mohammed regarded the Jewish and Christian tribes in Arabia as exceptions to the rule that an ethnical group (*ummah*) was at the same time a religious unity. He did not imagine that it could be in Allah's plan that the Arabs were to conform to a revelation given in a foreign language. No; God must speak to them in Arabic[8]. Through whose mouth?

A long and severe crisis preceded Mohammed's call. He was convinced that, if he were the man, mighty signs from Heaven must be revealed to him, for his con-

---

7   *Qoran*, xxxii., 2; xxxiv., 43; xxxvi., 5, etc.
8   *Ibid*., xii., 2; xiii., 37; XX., 112; XXVI., 195; xli., 44, etc.

ception of revelation was mechanical; Allah Himself, or at least angels, must speak to him. The time of waiting, the process of objectifying the subjective, lived through by the help of an overstrained imagination, all this laid great demands upon the psychical and physical constitution of Mohammed. At length he saw and heard that which he thought he ought to hear and see. In feverish dreams he found the form for the revelation, and he did not in the least realize that the contents of his inspiration from Heaven were nothing but the result of what he had himself absorbed. He realized it so little, that the identity of what was revealed to him with what he held to be the contents of the Scriptures of Jews and Christians was a miracle to him, the only miracle upon which he relied for the support of his mission.

In the course of the twenty-three years of Mohammed's work as God's messenger, the over-excited state, or inspiration, or whatever we may call the peculiar spiritual condition in which his revelation was born, gradually gave place to quiet reflection. Especially after the Hijrah, when the prophet had to provide the state established by him at Medina with inspired regulations, the words of God became in almost every respect different from what they had been at first. Only the form was retained. In connection with this evolution, some of our biographers of Mohammed, even where they do not deny the obvious honesty of his first visions, represent him in the second half of his work, as a sort of actor, who played with that which had been most sacred to him. This accusation is, in my opinion, unjust.

Mohammed, who twelve years long, in spite of derision and contempt, continued to inveigh in the name of Allah against the frivolous conservatism of the heathens in Mecca, to preach Allah's omnipotence to them, to hold up to them Allah's commands and His promises and threats regarding the future life, "without asking any reward" for such exhausting work, is really not another man than the acknowledged "Messenger of Allah" in Medina, who saw his power gradually increase, who was taught by experience the value and the use of the material means of extending it, and who finally, by the force of arms compelled all Arabs to "obedience to Allah and His messenger."

In our own society, real enthusiasm in the propagation of an idea generally considered as absurd, if crowned by success may, in the course of time, end in cold, prosaic calculation without a trace of hypocrisy. Nowhere in the life of Mohammed can a point of turning be shown; there is a gradual changing of aims and a readjustment of the means of attaining them. From the first the outcast felt himself superior to the well-to-do people who looked down upon him; and with all his power he sought for a position from which he could force them to acknowledge his superiority. This he found in the next and better world, of which the Jews and Christians knew. After a crisis, which some consider as psychopathologic, he knew himself to be sent by Allah to call the materialistic community, which he hated and despised, to the alternative, either in following him to find eternal blessedness, or in denying him to be doomed to eternal fire.

Powerless against the scepticism of his hearers, after twelve years of preaching followed only by a few dozen, most of them outcasts like himself, he hoped now and then that Allah would strike the recalcitrant multitude with an earthly doom, as he knew from revelations had happened before. This hope was also unfulfilled. As other messengers of God had done in similar circumstances, he sought for a more fruitful field than that of his birthplace; he set out on the Hijrah, *i.e.*, emigration to Medina. Here circumstances were more favourable to him: in a short time he became the head of a considerable community.

Allah, who had given him power, soon allowed him to use it for the protection of the interests of the Faithful against the unbelievers. Once become militant, Mohammed turned from the purely defensive to the aggressive attitude, with such success that a great part of the Arab tribes were compelled to accept Islam, "obedience to Allah and His Messenger." The rule formerly insisted upon: "No compulsion in religion," was sacrificed, since experience taught him, that the truth was more easily forced upon men by violence than by threats which would be fulfilled only after the resurrection. Naturally, the religious value of the conversions sank in proportion as their number increased. The Prophet of world renouncement in Mecca wished to win souls for his faith; the Prophet-Prince in Medina needed subjects and fighters for his army. Yet he was still the same Mohammed.

Parallel with his altered position towards the heathen Arabs went a readjustment of his point of view towards the followers of Scripture. Mohammed never pretended to preach a new religion; he demanded in the name of Allah the same Islam (submission) that Moses, Jesus, and former prophets had demanded of their nations. In his earlier revelations he always points out the identity of his "Qorans" with the contents of the sacred books of Jews and Christians, in the sure conviction that these will confirm his assertion if asked. In Medina he was disillusioned by finding neither Jews nor Christians prepared to acknowledge an Arabian prophet, not even for the Arabs only; so he was led to distinguish between the *true* contents of the Bible and that which had been made of it by the falsification of later Jews and Christians. He preferred now to connect his own revelations more immediately with those of Abraham, no books of whom could be cited against him, and who was acknowledged by Jews and Christians without being himself either a Jew or a Christian.

This turn, this particular connection of Islam with Abraham, made it possible for him, by means of an adaptation of the biblical legends concerning Abraham, Hagar, and Ishmael, to include in his religion a set of religious customs of the Meccans, especially the hajj[9]. Thus Islam became more Arabian, and at the same time more independent of the other revealed religions, whose degeneracy was demonstrated by their refusal to acknowledge Mohammed.

All this is to be explained without the supposition of conscious trickery or dishonesty on the part of Mohammed. There was no other way for the unlettered Prophet, whose belief in his mission was unshaken, to overcome the difficulties entailed by his closer acquaintance with the tenets of other religions.

How, then, are we to explain the starting-point of it all—Mohammed's sense of vocation? Was it a disease of the spirit, a kind of madness? At all events, the data are insufficient upon which to form a serious diagnosis. Some have called it epilepsy. Sprenger, with an exaggerated display of certainty based upon his former medical studies, gave Mohammed's disorder the name of hysteria. Others try to find a connection between Mohammed's extraordinary interest in the fair sex and his prophetic consciousness. But, after all, is it explaining the spiritual life of a man, who was certainly unique, if we put a label upon him, and thus class him with others, who at the most shared with him certain abnormalities? A normal man Mohammed certainly was not. But as soon as we try to give a positive name to this negative quality, then we do the same as the heathens of Mecca, who were violently awakened by his thundering prophecies: "He is nothing but one possessed, a poet,

---

9 A complete explanation of the gradual development of the Abraham legend in the Qoran can be found in my book *Het Mekkaansche Feest* (The Feast of Mecca), Leiden, 1880.

a soothsayer, a sorcerer," they said. Whether we say with the old European biographers "impostor," or with the modern ones put "epileptic," or "hysteric" in its place, makes little difference. The Meccans ended by submitting to him, and conquering a world under the banner of his faith. We, with the diffidence which true science implies, feel obliged merely to call him Mohammed, and to seek in the Qoran, and with great cautiousness in the Tradition, a few principal points of his life and work, in order to see how in his mind the intense feeling of discontent during the misery of his youth, together with a great self-reliance, a feeling of spiritual superiority to his surroundings, developed into a call, the form of which was largely decided by Jewish and Christian influence.

While being struck by various weaknesses which disfigured this great personality and which he himself freely confessed, we must admire the perseverance with which he retained his faith in his divine mission, not discouraged by twelve years of humiliation, nor by the repudiation of the "People of Scripture," upon whom he had relied as his principal witnesses, nor yet by numbers of temporary rebuffs during his struggle for the dominion of Allah and His Messenger, which he carried on through the whole of Arabia.

Was Mohammed conscious of the universality of his mission? In the beginning he certainly conceived his work as merely the Arabian part of a universal task, which, for other parts of the world, was laid upon other messengers. In the Medina period he ever more decidedly chose the direction of "forcing to comply." He was content only when the heathens perceived that further resistance to Allah's hosts was useless; their understanding of his "clear Arabic Qoran" was no longer the principal object of his striving. *Such an Islam could equally well be forced upon* non-Arabian heathens. And, as regards the "People of Scripture," since Mohammed's endeavour to be recognized by them had failed, he had taken up his position opposed to them, even above them. With the rise of his power he became hard and cruel to the Jews in North-Arabia, and from Jews and Christians alike in Arabia he demanded submission to his authority, since it had proved impossible to make them recognize his divine mission. This demand could quite logically be extended to all Christians; in the first place to those of the Byzantine Empire. But did Mohammed himself come to these conclusions in the last part of his life? Are the words in which Allah spoke to him: "We have sent thee to men in general,"[10] and a few expressions of the same sort, to be taken in that sense, or does "humanity" here, as in many other places in the Qoran, mean those with whom Mohammed had especially to do? Noldeke is strongly of opinion that the principal lines of the program of conquest carried out after Mohammed's death, had been drawn by the Prophet himself. Lammens and others deny with equal vigour, that Mohammed ever looked upon the whole world as the field of his mission. This shows that the solution is not evident.[11]

In our valuation of Mohammed's sayings we cannot lay too much stress upon his incapability of looking far ahead. The final aims which Mohammed set himself were considered by sane persons as unattainable. His firm belief in the realization

---

10   *Qoran*, xxxiv., 27. The translation of this verse has always been a subject of great difference of opinion. At the time of its revelation — as fixed by Mohammedan as well as by western authorities — the universal conception of Mohammed's mission was quite out of question.

11   Professor T. W. Arnold in the 2d edition (London, 1913) of his valuable work *The Preaching of Islam* (especially pp. 28-31), warmly endeavours to prove that Mohammed from the beginning considered his mission as universal. He weakens his argument more than is necessary by placing the Tradition upon an almost equal footing with the Qoran as a source, and by ignoring the historical development which is obvious in the Qoran itself. In this way he does not perceive the great importance of the history of the Abraham legend in Mohammed's conception. Moreover, the translation of the verses of the Qoran on p. 29 sometimes says more than the original. Lil-nas is not "*to mankind*" but "*to men*," in the sense of "*to everybody*." Qoran, xvi., 86, does not say: "One day we will raise up a witness out of every nation," but: "On the day (*i.e.*, the day of resurrection) when we will raise up, etc.," which would seem to refer to the theme so constantly repeated in the Qoran, that each nation will be confronted on the Day of Judgment with the prophet sent to it. When the Qoran is called an "admonition to the world ('alamin)" and Mohammed's mission a "mercy to the world ('alamin)," then we must remember that 'alamin is one of the most misused rhymewords in the Qoran (e.g., Qoran, xv., 70); and we should not therefore translate it emphatically as "all created beings," unless the universality of Mohammed's mission is firmly established by other proofs. And this is far from being the case.

of the vague picture of the future which he had conceived, nay, which Allah held before him, drove him to the uttermost exertion of his mental power in order to surmount the innumerable unexpected obstacles which he encountered. Hence the variability of the practical directions contained in the Qoran; they are constantly altered according to circumstances. Allah's words during the last part of Mohammed's life: "This day have I perfected your religion for you, and have I filled up the measure of my favours towards you, and chosen Islam for you as your religion," have in no way the meaning of the exclamation: "It is finished," of the dying Christ. They are only a cry of jubilation over the degradation of the heathen Arabs by the triumph of Allah's weapons. At Mohammed's death everything was still unstable; and the vital questions for Islam were subjects of contention between the leaders even before the Prophet had been buried.

The expedient of new revelations completing, altering, or abrogating former ones had played an important part in the legislative work of Mohammed. Now, he had never considered that by his death the spring would be stopped, although completion was wanted in every respect. For, without doubt, Mohammed felt his weakness in systematizing and his absence of clearness of vision into the future, and therefore he postponed the promulgation of divine decrees as long as possible, and he solved only such questions of law as frequently recurred, when further hesitation would have been dangerous to his authority and to the peace of the community.

At Mohammed's death, all Arabs were not yet subdued to his authority. The expeditions which he had undertaken or arranged beyond the northern boundaries of Arabia, were directed against Arabs, although they were likely to rouse conflict with the Byzantine and Persian empires. It would have been contrary to Mohammed's usual methods if this had led him to form a general definition of his attitude towards the world outside Arabia.

As little as Mohammed, when he invoked the Meccans in wild poetic inspirations to array themselves behind him to seek the blessedness of future life, had dreamt of the possibility that twenty years later the whole of Arabia would acknowledge his authority in this world, as little, nay, much less, could he at the close of his life have had the faintest premonition of the fabulous development which his state would reach half a century later. The subjugation of the mighty Persia and of some of the richest provinces of the Byzantine Empire, only to mention these, was never a part of his program, although legend has it that he sent out written challenges to the six princes of the world best known to him. Yet we may say that Mohammed's successors in the guidance of his community, by continuing their expansion towards the north, after the suppression of the apostasy that followed his death, remained in Mohammed's line of action. There is even more evident continuity in the development of the empire of the Omayyads out of the state of Mohammed, than in the series of events by which we see the dreaded Prince-Prophet of Medina grew out of the "possessed one" of Mecca. But if Mohammed had been able to foresee how the unity of Arabia, which he nearly accomplished, was to bring into being a formidable international empire, we should expect some indubitable traces of this in the Qoran; not a few verses of dubious interpretation, but some certain sign that the Revelation, which had repeatedly, and with the greatest emphasis, called itself a "plain Arabic Qoran" intended for those "to whom no warner had yet been sent," should in future be valid for the 'Ajam, the Barbarians, as well as for the Arabs.

Even if we ascribe to Mohammed something of the universal program, which the later tradition makes him to have drawn up, he certainly could not foresee the success of it. For this, in the first place, the economic and political factors to which some scholars of our day would attribute the entire explanation of the Islam movement, must be taken into consideration. Mohammed did to some extent prepare the universality of his religion and make it possible. But that Islam, which came into the world as the Arabian form of the one, true religion, has actually become a universal religion, is due to circumstances which had little to do with its origin[12]. This extension of the domain to be subdued to its spiritual rule entailed upon Islam about three centuries of development and accommodation, of a different sort, to be sure, but not less drastic in character than that of the Christian Church.

---

12   Sir William Muir was not wrong when he said: "From first to last the summons was to Arabs and to none other... The seed of a universal creed had indeed been sown; but that it ever germinated was due to circumstances rather than design."

II

The Religious Development Of Islam

WE can hardly imagine a poorer, more miserable population than that of the South-Arabian country Hadramaut. All moral and social progress is there impeded by the continuance of the worst elements of Jahiliyyah (Arabian paganism), side by side with those of Islam. A secular nobility is formed by groups of people, who grudge each other their very lives and fight each other according to the rules of retaliation unmitigated by any more humane feelings. The religious nobility is represented by descendants of the Prophet, arduous patrons of a most narrow-minded orthodoxy and of most bigoted fanaticism. In a well-ordered society, making the most of all the means offered by modern technical science, the dry barren soil might be made to yield sufficient harvests to satisfy the wants of its members; but among these inhabitants, paralysed by anarchy, chronic famine prevails. Foreigners wisely avoid this miserable country, and if they did visit it, would not be hospitably received. Hunger forces many Hadramites to emigrate; throughout the centuries we find them in all the countries of Islam, in the sacred cities of Western-Arabia, in Syria, Egypt, India, Indonesia, where they often occupy important positions.

In the Dutch Indies, for instance, they live in the most important commercial towns, and though the Government has never favoured them, and though they have had to compete with Chinese and with Europeans, they have succeeded in making their position sufficiently strong. Before European influence prevailed, they even founded states in some of the larger islands or they obtained political influence in existing native states. Under a strong European government they are among the quietest, most industrious subjects, all earning their own living and saving something for their poor relations at home. They come penniless, and without any of that theoretical knowledge or practical skill which we are apt to consider as indispensable for a man who wishes to try his fortune in a complicated modern colonial world. Yet I have known some who in twenty years' time have become commercial potentates, and even millionaires.

The strange spectacle of these latent talents and of the suppressed energy of the people of Hadramaut that seem to be waiting only for transplantation into a more favourable soil to develop with amazing rapidity, helps us to understand the enormous consequences of the Arabian migration in the seventh century.

The spiritual goods, with which Islam set out into the world, were far from imposing. It preached a most simple monotheism: Allah, the Almighty Creator and Ruler of heaven and earth, entirely self-sufficient, so that it were ridiculous to suppose Him to have partners or sons and daughters to support Him; who has created the angels that they might form His retinue, and men and genii (jinn) that they might obediently serve Him; who decides everything according to His incalculable will and is responsible to nobody, as the Universe is His; of whom His creatures, if their minds be not led astray, must therefore stand in respectful fear and awe. He has made His will known to mankind, beginning at Adam, but the spreading of mankind over the surface of the earth, its seduction by Satan and his emissaries have caused most nations to become totally estranged from Him and His service. Now and then, when He considered that the time was come, He caused a prophet to arise from among a nation to be His messenger to summon people to conversion, and to tell them what blessedness awaited them as a reward of obedience, what punishments would be inflicted if they did not believe his message.

Sometimes the disobedient had been struck by earthly judgment (the flood, the drowning of the Egyptians, etc.), and the faithful had been rescued in a miraculous way and led to victory; but such things merely served as indications of Allah's greatness. One day the whole world will be overthrown and destroyed. Then the dead will be awakened and led before Allah's tribunal. The faithful will have abodes appointed them in well-watered, shady gardens, with fruit-trees richly laden, with luxurious couches upon which they may lie and enjoy the delicious food, served by the ministrants of Paradise. They may also freely indulge in sparkling wine that does not intoxicate, and in intercourse with women, whose youth and virginity do not fade. The unbelievers end their lives in Hell-fire; or, rather, there is no end, for the punishment as well as the reward are everlasting.

Allah gives to each one his due. The actions of His creatures are all accurately written down, and when judgment comes, the book is opened; moreover, every creature carries the list of his own deeds and misdeeds; the debit and credit sides are carefully weighed against each other in the divine scales, and many witnesses are heard before judgment is pronounced. Allah, however, is clement and merciful; He gladly forgives those sinners who have believed in Him, who have sincerely accepted Islam, that is to say: who have acknowledged His absolute authority and have believed the message of the prophet sent to them. These prophets have the privilege of acting as mediators on behalf of their followers, not in the sense of redeemers, but as advocates who receive gracious hearing.

Naturally, Islam, submission to the Lord of the Universe, ought to express itself in deeds. Allah desires the homage of formal worship, which must be performed several times a day by every individual, and on special occasions by the assembled faithful, led by one of them. This. service, [s.]alat, acquired its strictly binding rules only after Mohammed's time, but already in his lifetime it consisted chiefly of the same elements as now: the recital of sacred texts, especially taken from the Revelation, certain postures of the body (standing, inclination, kneeling, prostration) with the face towards Mecca. This last particular and the language of the Revelation are the Arabian elements of the service, which is for the rest an imitation of Jewish and Christian rituals, so far as Mohammed knew them. There was no sacrament, consequently no priest to administer it; Islam has always been the lay religion *par excellence*. Teaching and exhortation are the only spiritual help that the pious Mohammedan wants, and this simple care of souls is exercised without any ordination or consecration.

Fasting, for a month if possible, and longer if desired, was also an integral part of religious life and, by showing disregard of earthly joys, a proof of faith in Allah's promises for the world to come. Almsgiving, recommended above all other virtues, was not only to be practised in obedience to Allah's law and in faith in retribution, but it was to testify contempt of all earthly possessions which might impede the striving after eternal happiness. Later, Mohammed was compelled, by the need of a public fund and the waning zeal of the faithful as their numbers increased, to regulate the practice of this virtue and to exact certain minima as taxes (*zakat*).

When Mohammed, taking his stand as opposed to Judaism and Christianity, had accentuated the Arabian character of his religion, the Meccan rites of pagan origin were incorporated into Islam; but only after the purification required by monotheism. From that time forward the yearly celebration of the Hajj was among the ritual duties of the Moslim community.

In the first years of the strife yet another duty was most emphatically impressed on the Faithful; jihad, i.e., readiness to sacrifice life and possessions for the defence of Islam, understood, since the conquest of Mecca in 630, as the extension by force of arms of the authority of the Moslim state, first over the whole of Arabia, and soon after Mohammed's death over the whole world, so far as Allah granted His hosts the victory.

For the rest, the legislative revelations regulated only such points as had become subjects of argument or contest in Mohammed's lifetime, or such as were particularly suggested by that antithesis of paganism and revelation, which had determined Mohammed's prophetical career. Gambling and wine were forbidden, the latter after some hesitation between the inculcation of temperance and that of abstinence. Usury, taken in the sense of requiring any interest at all upon loans, was also forbidden. All tribal feuds with their consequences had henceforward to be considered as non-existent, and retaliation, provided that the offended party would not agree to accept compensation, was put under the control of the head of the community. Polygamy and intercourse of master and female slave were restricted; the obligations arising from blood-relationship or ownership were regulated. These points suffice to remind us of the nature of the Qoranic regulations. Reference to certain subjects in this revealed law while others were ignored, did not depend on their respective importance to the life of the community, but rather on what happened to have been suggested by the events in Mohammed's lifetime. For Mohammed knew too well how little qualified he was for legislative work to undertake it unless absolutely necessary.

This rough sketch of what Islam meant when it set out to conquer the world, is not very likely to create the impression that its incredibly rapid extension was due to its superiority over the forms of civilization which it supplanted. Lammens's assertion, that Islam was the Jewish religion simplified according to Arabic wants and amplified by some Christian and Arabic traditions, contains a great deal of truth, if only we recognize the central importance for Mohammed's vocation and preaching of the Christian doctrine of Resurrection and judgment. This explains the large number of weak points that the book of Mohammed's revelations, written down by his first followers, offered to Jewish and Christian polemics. It was easy for the theologians of those religions to point out numberless mistakes in the work of the illiterate Arabian prophet, especially where he maintained that he was repeating and confirming the contents of their Bible. The Qoranic revelations about Allah's intercourse with men, taken from apocryphal sources, from profane legends like that of Alexander the Great, sometimes even created by Mohammed's own fancy—such as the story of the prophet Salih, said to have lived in the north of Arabia, and that of the prophet Hud, supposed to have lived in the south; all this could not but give them the impression of a clumsy caricature of true tradition. The principal doctrines of Synagogue and Church had apparently been misunderstood, or they were simply denied as corruptions.

The conversion to Islam, within a hundred years, of such nations as the Egyptian, the Syrian, and the Persian, can hardly be attributed to anything but the latent talents, the formerly suppressed energy of the Arabian race having found a favourable soil for its development; talents and energy, however, not of a missionary kind. If Islam is said to have been from its beginning down to the present day, a missionary religion,[13] then "mission" is to be taken here in a quite peculiar sense, and special attention must be given to the preparation of the missionary field by the Moslim armies, related by history and considered as most important by the

---

13 With extraordinary talent this thesis has been defended by Professor T.W. Arnold in the above quoted work, *The Preaching of Islam*, which fully deserves the attention also of those who do not agree with the writer's argument. Among the many objections that may be raised against Prof. Arnold's conclusion, we point to the undeniable fact, that the Moslim scholars of all ages hardly speak of "mission" at all, and always treat the extension of the true faith by holy war as one of the principal duties of the Moslim community.

Mohammedans themselves.

Certainly, the nations conquered by the Arabs under the first khalifs were not obliged to choose between living as Moslims or dying as unbelievers. The conquerors treated them as Mohammed had treated Jews and Christians in Arabia towards the end of his life, and only exacted from them submission to Moslim authority. They were allowed to adhere to their religion, provided they helped with their taxes to fill the Moslim exchequer. This rule was even extended to such religions as that of the Parsis, although they could not be considered as belonging to the "People of Scripture" expressly recognized in the Qoran. But the social condition of these subjects was gradually made so oppressive by the Mohammedan masters, that rapid conversions in masses were a natural consequence; the more natural because among the conquered nations intellectual culture was restricted to a small circle, so that after the conquest their spiritual leaders lacked freedom of movement. Besides, practically very little was required from the new converts, so that it was very tempting to take the step that led to full citizenship.

No, those who in a short time subjected millions of non-Arabs to the state founded by Mohammed, and thus prepared their conversion, were no apostles. They were generals whose strategic talents would have remained hidden but for Mohammed, political geniuses, especially from Mecca and Taif, who, before Islam, would have excelled only in the organization of commercial operations or in establishing harmony between hostile families. Now they proved capable of uniting the Arabs commanded by Allah, a unity still many a time endangered during the first century by the old party spirit; and of devising a division of labour between the rulers and the conquered which made it possible for them to control the function of complicated machines of state without any technical knowledge.

Moreover, several circumstances favoured their work; both the large realms which extended north of Arabia, were in a state of political decline; the Christians inhabiting the provinces that were to be conquered first, belonged, for the larger part, to heretical sects and were treated by the orthodox Byzantines in such a way that other masters, if tolerant, might be welcome. The Arabian armies consisted of hardened Bedouins with few wants, whose longing for the treasures of the civilized world made them more ready to endure the pressure of a discipline hitherto unknown to them.

The use that the leaders made of the occasion commands our admiration; although their plan was formed in the course and under the influence of generally unforeseen events. Circumstances had changed Mohammed the Prophet into Mohammed the Conqueror; and the leaders, who continued the conqueror's work, though not driven by fanaticism or religious zeal, still prepared the conversion of millions of men to Islam.

It was only natural that the new masters adopted, with certain modifications, the administrative and fiscal systems of the conquered countries. For similar reasons Islam had to complete its spiritual store from the well-ordered wealth of that of its new adherents. Recent research shows most clearly, that Islam, in after times so sharply opposed to other religions and so strongly armed against foreign influence, in the first century borrowed freely and simply from the "People of Scripture" whatever was not evidently in contradiction to the Qoran. This was to be expected; had not Mohammed from the very beginning referred to the "people of the Book" as "those who know"? When painful experience induced him afterwards to accuse them of corruption of their Scriptures, this attitude necessitated a certain criticism but not rejection of their tradition. The ritual, only provisionally regulated and continually liable to change according to prophetic inspiration in Mohammed's lifetime, required unalterable rules after his death. Recent studies[14] have shown in an astounding way, that the Jewish ritual, together with the religious rites of the Christians, strongly influenced the definite shape given to that of Islam, while indirect influence of the Parsi religion is at least probable.

So much for the rites of public worship and the ritual purity they require. The method of fasting seems to follow the Jewish model, whereas the period of obligatory fasting depends on the Christian usage.

Mohammed's fragmentary and unsystematic accounts of sacred history were freely drawn from Jewish and Christian sources and covered the whole period from the creation of the world until the first centuries of the Christian era. Of course, features shocking to the Moslim mind were dropped and the whole adapted to the monotonous conception of the Qoran. With ever greater boldness the story of Mo-

---

14   The studies of Professors C.H. Becker, E. Mittwoch, and A.J. Wensinck, especially taken in connection with older ones of Ignaz Goldziher, have thrown much light upon this subject.

hammed's own life was exalted to the sphere of the supernatural; here the Gospel served as example. Though Mohammed had repeatedly declared himself to be an ordinary man chosen by Allah as the organ of His revelation, and whose only miracle was the Qoran, posterity ascribed to him a whole series of wonders, evidently invented in emulation of the wonders of Christ. The reason for this seems to have been the idea that none of the older prophets, not even Jesus, of whom the Qoran tells the greatest wonders, could have worked a miracle without Mohammed, the Seal of the prophets, having rivalled or surpassed him in this respect. Only Jesus was the Messiah; but this title did not exceed in value different titles of other prophets, and Mohammed's special epithets were of a higher order. A relative sinlessness Mohammed shared with Jesus; the acceptance of this doctrine, contradictory to the original spirit of the Qoran, had moreover a dogmatic motive: it was considered indispensable to raise the text of the Qoran above all suspicion of corruption, which suspicion would not be excluded if the organ of the Revelation were fallible.

This period of naively adopting institutions, doctrines, and traditions was soon followed by an awakening to the consciousness that Islam could not well absorb any more of such foreign elements without endangering its independent character. Then a sorting began; and the assimilation of the vast amount of borrowed matter, that had already become an integral part of Islam, was completed by submitting the whole to a peculiar treatment. It was carefully divested of all marks of origin and labelled *hadith*[15], so that henceforth it was regarded as emanations from the wisdom of the Arabian Prophet, for which his followers owed no thanks to foreigners.

At first, it was only at Medina that some pious people occupied themselves with registering, putting in order, and systematizing the spiritual property of Islam; afterwards similar circles were formed in other centres, such as Mecca, Kufa, Basra, Misr (Cairo), and elsewhere. At the outset the collection of divine sayings, the Qoran, was the only guide, the only source of decisive decrees, the only touchstone of what was true or false, allowed or forbidden. Reluctantly, but decidedly at last, it was conceded that the foundations laid by Mohammed for the life of his commu-

---

15 *Hadith*, the Arabic word for record, story, has assumed the technical meaning of "tradition" concerning the words and deeds of Mohammed. It is used as well in the sense of a single record of this sort as in that of the whole body of sacred traditions.

nity were by no means all to be found in the Holy Book; rather, that Mohammed's revelations without his explanation and practice would have remained an enigma. It was understood now that the rules and laws of Islam were founded on God's word and on the Sunnah, *i.e.*, the "way" pointed out by the Prophet's word and example. Thus it had been from the moment that Allah had caused His light to shine over Arabia, and thus it must remain, if human error was not to corrupt Islam.

At the moment when this conservative instinct began to assert itself among the spiritual leaders, so much foreign matter had already been incorporated into Islam, that the theory of the sufficiency of Qoran and Sunnah could not have been maintained without the labelling operation which we have alluded to. So it was assumed that as surely as Mohammed must have surpassed his predecessors in perfection and in wonders, so surely must all the principles and precepts necessary for his community have been formulated by him. Thus, by a gigantic web of fiction, he became after his death the organ of opinions, ideas, and interests, whose lawfulness was recognized by every influential section of the Faithful. All that could not be identified as part of the Prophet's Sunnah, received no recognition; on the other hand, all that was accepted had, somehow, to be incorporated into the Sunnah.

It became a fundamental dogma of Islam, that the Sunnah was the indispensable completion of the Qoran, and that both together formed the source of Mohammedan law and doctrine; so much so that every party assumed the name of "People of the Sunnah" to express its pretension to orthodoxy. The *contents* of the Sunnah, however, was the subject of a great deal of controversy; so that it came to be considered necessary to make the Prophet pronounce his authoritative judgment on this difference of opinion. He was said to have called it a proof of God's special mercy, that within reasonable limits difference of opinion was allowed in his community. Of that privilege Mohammedans have always amply availed themselves.

When the difference touched on political questions, especially on the succession of the Prophet in the government of the community, schism was the inevitable consequence. Thus arose the party strifes of the first century, which led to the establishment of the sects of the Shi'ites and the Kharijites, separate communities, severed from the great whole, that led their own lives, and therefore followed paths different from those of the majority in matters of doctrine and law as well as in politics. The sharpness of the political antithesis served to accentuate the importance of the other differences in such cases and to debar their acceptance as the legal consequence of the difference of opinion that God's mercy allowed. That the political factor was indeed the great motive of separation, is clearly shown in our own day, now that one Mohammedan state after the other sees its political independence disappearing and efforts are being made from all sides to re-establish the unity of the Mohammedan world by stimulating the feeling of religious brotherhood. Among the most cultivated Moslims of different countries an earnest endeavour is gaining ground to admit Shi'ites, Kharijites, and others, formerly abused as heretics, into the great community, now threatened by common foes, and to regard their special tenets in the same way as the differences existing between the four law schools: Hanafites, Malikites, Shafi'ites and Hanbalites, which for centuries have been considered equally orthodox.

Although the differences that divide these schools at first caused great excitement and gave rise to violent discussions, the strong catholic instinct of Islam always knew how to prevent schism. Each new generation either found the golden mean between the extremes which had divided the preceding one, or it recognized the right of both opinions.

Though the dogmatic differences were not necessarily so dangerous to unity as were political ones, yet they were more apt to cause schism than discussions about the law. It was essential to put an end to dissension concerning the theological roots of the whole system of Islam. Mohammed had never expressed any truth in dogmatic form; all systematic thinking was foreign to his nature. It was again the non-Arabic Moslims, especially those of Christian origin, who suggested such doctrinal questions. At first they met with a vehement opposition that condemned all dogmatic discussion as a novelty of the Devil. In the long run, however, the contest of the conservatives against specially objectionable features of the dogmatists' discussions forced them to borrow arms from the dogmatic arsenal. Hence a method with a peculiar terminology came in vogue, to which even the boldest imagination could not ascribe any connection with the Sunnah of Mohammed. Yet some traditions ventured to put prophetic warnings on Mohammed's lips against dogmatic innovations that were sure to arise, and to make him pronounce the names of a couple of future sects. But no one dared to make the Prophet preach an orthodox system of dogmatics resulting from the controversies of several centuries, all the terms of which were foreign to the Arabic speech of Mohammed's time.

Indeed, all the subjects which had given rise to dogmatic controversy in the Christian Church, except some too specifically Christian, were discussed by the *mutakallims*, the dogmatists of Islam. Free will or predestination; God omnipotent, or first of all just and holy; God's word created by Him, or sharing His eternity; God one in this sense, that His being admitted of no plurality of qualities, or possessed of qualities, which in all eternity are inherent in His being; in the world to come only bliss and doom, or also an intermediate state for the neutral. We might continue the enumeration and always show to the Christian church-historian or theologian old acquaintances in Moslim garb. That is why Maracci and Reland could understand Jews and Christians yielding to the temptation of joining Islam, and that also explains why Catholic and Protestant dogmatists could accuse each other of Crypto-mohammedanism.

Not until the beginning of the tenth century A.D. did the orthodox Mohammedan dogma begin to emerge from the clash of opinions into its definite shape. The Mu'tazilites had advocated man's free will; had given prominence to justice and holiness in their conception of God, had denied distinct qualities in God and the eternity of God's Word; had accepted a place for the neutral between Paradise and Hell; and for some time the favour of the powers in authority seemed to assure the victory of their system. Al-Ash'ari contradicted all these points, and his system has in the end been adopted by the great majority. The Mu'tazilite doctrines for a long time still enthralled many minds, but they ended by taking refuge in the political heresy of Shi'itism. In the most conservative circles, opponents to all speculation were never wanting; but they were obliged unconsciously to make large concessions to systematic thought; for in the Moslim world as elsewhere religious belief without dogma had become as impossible as breathing is without air.

Thus, in Islam, a whole system, which could not even pretend to draw its authority from the Sunnah, had come to be accepted. It was not difficult to justify this deviation from the orthodox abhorrence against novelties. Islam has always looked at the world in a pessimistic way, a view expressed in numberless prophetic sayings. The world is bad and will become worse and worse. Religion and morality will have to wage an ever more hopeless war against unbelief, against heresy and ungodly ways of living. While this is surely no reason for entering into any compromise with doctrines which depart but a hair's breadth from Qoran and Sunnah, it necessitates methods of defence against heresy as unknown in Mohammed's time as heresy itself. "Necessity knows no law" is a principle fully accepted in Islam; and heresy is an enemy of the faith that can only be defeated with dialectic weapons. So the religious truths preached by Mohammed have not been altered in any way; but under the stress of necessity they have been clad in modern armour, which has somewhat changed their aspect.

Moreover, Islam has a theory, which alone is sufficient to justify the whole later development of doctrine as well as of law. This theory, whose importance for the system can hardly be overestimated, and which, nevertheless, has until very recent times constantly been overlooked by Western students of Islam, finds its classical expression in the following words, put into the mouth of Mohammed: "My community will never agree in an error." In terms more familiar to us, this means that the Mohammedan Church taken as a whole is infallible; that all the decisions on matters practical or theoretical, on which it is agreed, are binding upon its members. Nowhere else is the catholic instinct of Islam more clearly expressed.

A faithful Mohammedan student, after having struggled through a handbook of law, may be vexed by a doubt as to whether these endless casuistic precepts have been rightly deduced from the Qoran and the Sacred Tradition. His doubt, however, will at once be silenced, if he bears in mind that Allah speaks more plainly to him by this infallible Agreement (Ijma') of the Community than through Qoran and Tradition; nay, that the contents of both those sacred sources, without this perfect intermediary, would be to a great extent unintelligible to him. Even the differences between the schools of law may be based on this theory of the Ijma'; for, does not the infallible Agreement of the Community teach us that a certain diversity of opinion is a merciful gift of God? It was through the Agreement that dogmatic speculations as well as minute discussions about points of law became legitimate. The stamp of Ijma' was essential to every rule of faith and life, to all manners and customs.

All sorts of religious ideas and practices, which could not possibly be deduced from Mohammed's message, entered the Moslim world by the permission of Ijma'. Here we need think only of mysticism and of the cult of saints.

Some passages of the Qoran may perhaps be interpreted in such a way that we hear the subtler strings of religious emotion vibrating in them. The chief impression that Mohammed's Allah makes before the Hijrah is that of awful majesty, at which men tremble from afar; they fear His punishment, dare hardly be sure of His reward, and hope much from His mercy. This impression is a lasting one; but, after the Hijrah, Allah is also heard quietly reasoning with His obedient servants, giving them advice and commands, which they have to follow in order to frustrate all resistance to His authority and to deserve His satisfaction. He is always the Lord, the King of the world, who speaks to His humble servants. But the lamp which Allah had caused Mohammed to hold up to guide mankind with its light, was raised higher and higher after the Prophet's death, in order to shed its light over an ever increasing part of humanity. This was not possible, however, without its reservoir being replenished with all the different kinds of oil that had from time immemorial given light to those different nations. The oil of mysticism came from Christian circles, and its Neo-Platonic origin was quite unmistakable; Persia and India also contributed to it. There were those who, by asceticism, by different methods of mortifying the flesh, liberated the spirit that it might rise and become united with the origin of all being; to such an extent, that with some the profession of faith was reduced to the blasphemous exclamation: "I am Allah." Others tried to become free from the sphere of the material and the temporal by certain methods of thought, combined or not combined with asceticism. Here the necessity of guidance was felt, and congregations came into existence, whose purpose it was to permit large groups of people under the leadership of their sheikhs, to participate simultaneously in the mystic union. The influence which spread most widely was that of leaders like Ghazali, the Father of the later Mohammedan Church, who recommended moral purification of the soul as the only way by which men should come nearer to God. His mysticism wished to avoid the danger of pantheism, to which so many others were led by their contemplations, and which so often engendered disregard of the revealed law, or even of morality. Some wanted to pass over the gap between the Creator and the created along a bridge of contemplation; and so, driven by the fire of sublime passion, precipitate themselves towards the object of their love, in a kind of rapture, which poets compare with intoxication. The evil world said that the impossibility to accomplish this heavenly union often induced those people to imitate it for the time being with the earthly means of wine and the indulgence in sensual love.

Characteristic of all these sorts of mysticism is their esoteric pride. All those emotions are meant only for a small number of chosen ones. Even Ghazali's ethical mysticism is not for the multitude. The development of Islam as a whole, from the Hijrah on, has always been greater in breadth than in depth; and, consequently, its pedagogics have remained defective. Even some of the noblest minds in Islam restrict true religious life to an aristocracy, and accept the ignorance of the multitude as an irremediable evil.

Throughout the centuries pantheistic and animistic forms of mysticism have found many adherents among the Mohammedans; but the infallible Agreement has persisted in calling that heresy. Ethical mysticism, since Ghazali, has been fully recognized; and, with law and dogma, it forms the sacred trio of sciences of Islam, to the study of which the Arabic humanistic arts serve as preparatory instruments. All other sciences, however useful and necessary, are of this world and have no value for the world to come. The unfaithful appreciate and study them as well as do the Mohammedans; but, on Mohammedan soil they must be coloured with a Mohammedan hue, and their results may never clash with the three religious sciences. Physics, astronomy, and philosophy have often found it difficult to observe this restriction, and therefore they used to be at least slightly suspected in pious circles.

Mysticism did not only owe to Ijma' its place in the sacred trio, but it succeeded, better than dogmatics, in confirming its right with words of Allah and His Prophet. In Islam mysticism and allegory are allied in the usual way; for the *illuminati* the words had quite a different meaning than for common, every-day people. So the Qoran was made to speak the language of mysticism; and mystic commentaries of the Holy Book exist, which, with total disregard for philological and historical objections, explain the verses of the Revelation as expressions of the profoundest soul experiences. Clear utterances in this spirit were put into the Prophet's mouth; and, like the canonists, the leaders on the mystic Way to God boasted of a spiritual genealogy which went back to Mohammed. Thus the Prophet is said to have declared void all knowledge and fulfillment of the law which lacks mystic experience.

Of course only "true" mysticism is justified by Ijma' and confirmed by the evidence of Qoran and Sunnah; but, about the bounds between "true" and "false" or heretical mysticism, there exists in a large measure the well-known diversity of opinion allowed by God's grace. The ethical mysticism of al-Ghazali is generally recognized as orthodox; and the possibility of attaining to a higher spiritual sphere by means of methodic asceticism and contemplation is doubted by few. The following opinion has come to prevail in wide circles: the Law offers the bread of life to all the faithful, the dogmatics are the arsenal from which the weapons must be taken to defend the treasures of religion against unbelief and heresy, but mysticism shows the earthly pilgrim the way to Heaven.

It was a much lower need that assured the cult of saints a place in the doctrine and practice of Islam. As strange as is Mohammed's transformation from an ordinary son of man, which he wanted to be, into the incarnation of Divine Light, as the later biographers represent him, it is still more astounding that the intercession of saints should have become indispensable to the community of Mohammed, who, according to Tradition, cursed the Jews and Christians because they worshipped the shrines of their prophets. Almost every Moslim village has its patron saint; every country has its national saints; every province of human life has its own human rulers, who are intermediate between the Creator and common mortals. In no other particular has Islam more fully accommodated itself to the religions it supplanted. The popular practice, which is in many cases hardly to be distinguished from polytheism, was, to a great extent, favoured by the theory of the intercession of the pious dead, of whose friendly assistance people might assure themselves by doing good deeds in their names and to their eternal advantage.

The ordinary Moslim visitor of the graves of saints does not trouble himself with this ingenious compromise between the severe monotheism of his prophet and the polytheism of his ancestors. He is firmly convinced, that the best way to obtain the satisfaction of his desire after earthly or heavenly goods is to give the saint whose special care these are what he likes best; and he confidently leaves it to the venerated one to settle the matter with Allah, who is far too high above the ordinary mortal to allow of direct contact.

In support even of this startling deviation from the original, traditions have been devised. Moreover, the veneration of human beings was favoured by some forms of mysticism; for, like many saints, many mystics had their eccentricities, and it was much to the advantage of mystic theologians if the vulgar could be persuaded to accept their aberrations from normal rules of life as peculiarities of holy men. But

Ijma' did more even than tradition and mysticism to make the veneration of legions of saints possible in the temples of the very men who were obliged by their ritual law to say to Allah several time daily: "Thee only do we worship and to Thee alone do we cry for help."

In the tenth century of our era Islam's process of accommodation was finished in all its essentials. From this time forward, if circumstances were favourable, it could continue the execution of its world conquering plans without being compelled to assimilate any more foreign elements. Against each spiritual asset that another universal religion could boast, it could now put forward something of a similar nature, but which still showed characteristics of its own, and the superiority of which it could sustain by arguments perfectly satisfactory to its followers. From that time on, Islam strove to distinguish itself ever more sharply from its most important rivals. There was no absolute stagnation, the evolution was not entirely stopped; but it moved at a much quieter pace, and its direction was governed by internal motives, not by influences from outside. Moslim catholicism had attained its full growth.

We cannot within the small compass of these lectures consider the excrescences of the normal Islam, the Shi'itic ultras, who venerated certain descendants of Mohammed as infallible rulers of the world, Ishma'ilites, Qarmatians, Assassins; nor the modern bastards of Islam, such as the Sheikhites, the Babi's, the Beha'is—who have found some adherents in America—and other sects, which indeed sprang up on Moslim soil, but deliberately turned to non-Mohammedan sources for their inspirations. We must draw attention, however, to protests raised by certain minorities against some of the ideas and practices which had been definitely adopted by the majority.

In the midst of Mohammedan Catholicism there always lived and moved more or less freely "protestant" elements. The comparison may even be continued, with certain qualifications, and we may speak also of a conservative and of a liberal protestantism in Islam. The conservative Protestantism is represented by the Hanbalitic school and kindred spirits, who most emphatically preached that the Agreement (Ijma') of every period should be based on that of the "pious ancestors." They therefore tested every dogma and practice by the words and deeds of the Prophet, his contemporaries, and the leaders of the Community in the first decades after Mohammed's death. In their eyes the Church of later days had degenerated; and they declined to consider the agreement of its doctors as justifying the penetration into Islam of ideas and usages of foreign origin. The cult of saints was rejected by them as altogether contradictory to the Qoran and the genuine tradition. These protestants of Islam may be compared to those of Christianity also in this respect, that they accepted the results of the evolution and assimilation of the first three centuries of Islam, but rejected later additions as abuse and corruption. When on the verge of our nineteenth century, they tried, as true Moslims, to force by material means their religious conceptions on others, they were combated as heretics by the authorities of catholic Islam. Central and Western Arabia formed the battlefield on which these zealots, called Wahhabites after their leader, were defeated by Mohammed Ali, the first Khedive, and his Egyptian army. Since they have given up their efforts at violent reconstitution of what they consider to be the original Islam, they are left alone, and their ideas have found adherents far outside Arabia, *e.g.*, in British India and in Northern and Central Africa.

In still quite another way many Moslims who found their freedom of thought or action impeded by the prevailing law and doctrine, have returned to the origin of their religion. Too much attached to the traditions of their faith, deliberately to disregard these impediments, they tried to find in the Qoran and Tradition arguments in favour of what was dictated to them by Reason; and they found those arguments as easily as former generations had found the bases on which to erect their casuistry, their dogma, and their mysticism. This implied an interpretation of the oldest sources independent from the catholic development of Islam, and in contradiction with the general opinion of the canonists, according to whom, since the fourth or fifth century of the Hijrah, no one is qualified for such free research. A certain degree of independence of mind, together with a strong attachment to their spiritual past, has given rise in the Moslim world to this sort of liberal protestantism, which in our age has many adherents among the Mohammedans who have come in contact with modern civilization.

That the partisans of all these different conceptions could remain together as the children of one spiritual family, is largely owing to the elastic character of Ijma', the importance of which is to some extent acknowledged by catholics and protestants, by moderns and conservatives. It has never been contested that the community, whose agreement was the test of truth, should not consist of the faithful masses, but of the expert elect. In a Christian church we should have spoken of the clergy, with a further definition of the organs through which it was to express itself synod, council, or Pope. Islam has no clergy, as we have seen; the qualification of a man to have his own opinion depends entirely upon the scope of his knowledge or rather of his erudition. There is no lack of standards, fixed by Mohammedan authorities, in which the requirements for a scholar to qualify him for Ijma' are detailed. The principal criterion is the knowledge of the canon law; quite what we should expect from the history of the evolution of Islam. But, of course, dogmatists and mystics had also their own "agreements" on the questions concerning them, and through the compromise between Law, Dogma, and Mysticism, there could not fail to come into existence a kind of mixed Ijma'. Moreover, the standards and definitions could have only a certain theoretical value, as there never has existed a body that could speak in the name of all. The decisions of Ijma' were therefore to be ascertained only in a vague and general way. The speakers were individuals whose own authority depended on Ijma', whereas Ijma' should have been their collective decision. Thus it was possible for innumerable shades of Catholicism and protestantism to live under one roof; with a good deal of friction, it is true, but without definite breach or schism, no one sect being able to eject another from the community.

Moslim political authorities are bound not only to extend the domain of Islam, but also to keep the community in the right path in its life and doctrine. This task they have always conceived in accordance with their political interests; Islam has had its religious persecutions but tolerance was very usual, and even official favouring of heresy not quite exceptional with Moslim rulers. Regular maintenance of religious discipline existed nowhere. Thus in the bond of political obedience elements which might otherwise have been scattered were held together. The political decay of Islam in our a day has done away with what had been left of official power to settle religious differences and any organization of spiritual authority never existed. Hence it is only natural that the diversity of opinion allowed by the grace of Allah now shows itself on a greater scale than ever before.

III

The Political Development Of Islam

IN the first period of Islam, the functions of what we call Church and what we call State were exercised by the same authority. Its political development is therefore of great importance for the understanding of its religious growth.

The Prophet, when he spoke in the name of God, was the lawgiver of his community, and it was rightly understood by the later Faithful that his indispensable explanations of God's word had also legislative power. From the time of the Hijrah the nature of the case made him the ruler, the judge, and the military commander of his theocratic state. Moreover, Allah expressly demanded of the Moslims that they should obey "the Messenger of God, and those amongst them who have authority."[16] We see by this expression that Mohammed shared his temporal authority with others. His co-rulers were not appointed, their number was nowhere defined, they were not a closed circle; they were the notables of the tribes or other groups who had arrayed themselves under Mohammed's authority, and a few who had gained influence by their personality. In their councils Mohammed's word had no decisive power, except when he spoke in the name of Allah; and we know how careful he was to give oracles only in cases of extreme need.

In the last years of Mohammed's life his authority became extended over a large part of Arabia; but he did very little in the way of centralization of government. He sent 'amils, i.e., agents, to the conquered tribes or villages, who had to see

16 Qoran, iv., 62.

that, in the first place, the most important regulations of the Qoran were followed, and, secondly, that the tax into which the duty of almsgiving had been converted was promptly paid, and that the portion of it intended for the central fund at Medina was duly delivered. After the great conquests, the governors of provinces of the Moslim Empire, who often exercised a despotic power, were called by the same title of 'amils. The agents of Mohammed, however, did not possess such unlimited authority. It was only gradually that the Arabs learned the value of good discipline and submission to a strong guidance, and adopted the forms of orderly government as they found them in the conquered lands.

Through the death of Mohammed everything became uncertain. The combination under one leadership of such a heterogeneous mass as that of his Arabs would have been unthinkable a few years before. It became quite natural, though, as soon as the Prophet's mouth was recognized as the organ of Allah's voice. Must this monarchy be continued after Allah's mouthpiece had ceased to exist? It was not at all certain. The force of circumstances and the energy of some of Mohammed's counsellors soon led to the necessary decisions. A number of the notables of the community succeeded in forcing upon the hesitating or unwilling members the acceptance of the monarchy as a permanent institution. There must be a khalif, a deputy of the Prophet in all his functions (except that of messenger of God), who would be ruler and judge and leader of public worship, but above all amir al-mu'minin, "Commander of the Faithful," in the struggle both against the apostate Arabs and against the hostile tribes on the northern border.

But for the military success of the first khalifs Islam would never have become a universal religion. Every exertion was made to keep the troops of the Faithful complete. The leaders followed only Mohammed's example when they represented fighting for Allah's cause as the most enviable occupation. The duty of military service was constantly impressed upon the Moslims; the lust of booty and the desire for martyrdom, to which the Qoran assigned the highest reward, were excited to the utmost. At a later period, it became necessary in the interests of order to temper the result of this excitement by traditions in which those of the Faithful who died in the exercise of a peaceful, honest profession were declared to be witnesses to the Faith as well as those who were slain in battle against the enemies of God,—traditions in which the real and greater holy war was described as the struggle against evil passions. The necessity of such a mitigating reaction, the spirit in which the chapters on holy war of Mohammedan lawbooks are conceived, and the galvanizing power which down to our own day is contained in a call to arms in the name of Allah, all this shows that in the beginning of Islam the love of battle had been instigated at the expense of everything else.

The institution of the Khalifate had hardly been agreed upon when the question of who should occupy it became the subject of violent dissension. The first four khalifs, whose reigns occupied the first thirty years after Mohammed's death, were Qoraishites, tribesmen of the Prophet, and moreover men who had been his intimate friends. The sacred tradition relates a saying of Mohammed: "The *imams* are from Qoraish," intended to confine the Khalifate to men from that tribe. History, however, shows that this edict was forged to give the stamp of legality to the results of a long political struggle. For at Mohammed's death the Medinese began fiercely contesting the claims of the Qoraishites; and during the reign of Ali, the fourth Khalif, the Kharijites rebelled, demanding, as democratic rigorists, the free election of khalifs without restriction to the tribe of Qoraish or to any other descent. Their standard of requirements contained only religious and moral qualities; and they claimed for the community the continual control of the chosen leader's behaviour and the right of deposing him as soon as they found him failing in the fulfilment of his duties. Their anarchistic revolutions, which during more than a century occasionally gave much trouble to the Khalifate, caused Islam to accentuate the aristocratic character of its monarchy. They were overcome and reduced to a sect, the survivors of which still exist in South-Eastern Arabia, in Zanzibar, and in Northern Africa; however, the actual life of these communities resembles that of their spiritual forefathers to a very remote degree.

Another democratic doctrine, still more radical than that of the Kharijites, makes even non-Arabs eligible for the Khalifate. It must have had a considerable number of adherents, for the tradition which makes the Prophet responsible for it is to be found in the canonic collections. Later generations, however, rendered it harmless by exegesis; they maintained that in this text "commander" meant only subordinate chiefs, and not "the Commander of the Faithful." It became a dogma in the orthodox Mohammedan world, respected up to the sixteenth century, that only members of the tribe of Qoraish could take the place of the Messenger of God.

The chance of success was greater for the legitimists than for the democratic party. The former wished to make the Khalifate the privilege of Ali, the cousin and son-in-law of the Prophet, and his descendants. At first the community did not take much notice of that "House of Mohammed"; and it did not occur to any one to give them a special part in the direction of affairs. Ali and Fatima themselves asked to be placed in possession only of certain goods which had belonged to Mohammed, but which the first khalifs would not allow to be regarded as his personal property; they maintained that the Prophet had had the disposal of them not as owner, but as head of the state. This narrow greed and absence of political insight seemed to be hereditary in the descendants of Ali and Fatima; for there was no lack of superstitious reverence for them in later times, and if one of them had possessed something of the political talent of the best Omayyads and Abbasids he would certainly have been able to supplant them.

After the third Khalif, Othman, had been murdered by his political opponents, Ali became his successor; but he was more remote than any of his predecessors from enjoying general sympathy. At that time the Shi'ah, the "Party" of the House of the Prophet, gradually arose, which maintained that Ali should have been the first Khalif, and that his descendants should succeed him. The veneration felt for those descendants increased in the same proportion as that for the Prophet himself; and moreover, there were at all times malcontents, whose advantage would be in joining any revolution against the existing government. Yet the Alids never succeeded in accomplishing anything against the dynasties of the Omayyads, the Abbasids, and the Ottomans, except in a few cases of transitory importance only.

The Fatimite dynasty, of rather doubtful descent, which ruled a part of Northern Africa and Egypt in the tenth century A.D., was completely suppressed after some two and a half centuries. The Sherifs who have ruled Morocco for more than 950 years were not chiefs of a party that considered the legality of their leadership a dogma; they owe their local Khalifate far more to the out-of-the-way position of their country which prevented Abbasids and Turks from meddling with their affairs. Otherwise, they would have been obliged at any rate to acknowledge the sovereignty of the Great Lord of Constantinople. This was the case with the Sherifs of Mecca, who ever since the twelfth century have regarded the sacred territory as their domain. Their principality arose out of the general political disturbance and the division of the Mohammedan empire into a number of kingdoms, whose mutual strife prevented them from undertaking military operations in the desert. These Sherifs raised no claim to the Khalifate; and the Shi'itic tendencies they displayed in the Middle Ages had no political significance, although they had intimate relations with the Zaidites of Southern Arabia. As first Egypt and afterwards Turkey made their protectorate over the holy cities more effective, the princes of Mecca became orthodox.

The Zaidites, who settled in Yemen from the ninth century on, are really Shi'ites, although of the most moderate kind. Without striving after expansion outside Arabia, they firmly refuse to give up their own Khalifate and to acknowledge the sovereignty of any non-Alid ruler; the efforts of the Turks to subdue them or to make a compromise with them have had no lasting results. This is the principal obstacle against their being included in the orthodox community, although their admission is defended, even under present circumstances, by many non-political Moslim scholars. The Zaidites are the remnant of the original Arabian Shi'ah, which for centuries has counted adherents in all parts of the Moslim world, and some of whose tenets have penetrated Mohammedan orthodoxy. The almost general veneration of the sayyids and sherifs, as the descendants of Mohammed are entitled, is due to this influence.

The Shi'ah outside Arabia, whose adherents used to be persecuted by the official authorities, not without good cause, became the receptacle of all the revolutionary and heterodox ideas maintained by the converted peoples. Alongside of the *visible* political history of Islam of the first centuries, these circles built up their evolution of the *unseen* community, the only true one, guided by the Holy Family, and the reality was to them a continuous denial of the postulates of religion. Their first *imam* or successor of the Prophet was Ali, whose divine right had been unjustly denied by the three usurpers, Abu Bakr, Omar, and Othman, and who had exercised actual authority for a few years in constant strife with Kharijites and Omayyads. The efforts of his legitimate successors to assert their authority were constantly drowned in blood; until, at last, there were no more candidates for the dangerous office. This prosaic fact was converted by the adherents of the House of Mohammed into the romance, that the last *imam of a line of seven* according to some, and *twelve* according to others, had disappeared in a mysterious way, to return at the end of days as Mahdi, the Guided One, who should restore the political order which had been disturbed ever since Mohammed's death. Until his reappearance there is nothing left for the community to do but to await his advent, under the guidance of their secular rulers (e.g., the shahs of Persia) and enlightened by their authoritative scholars (*mujtahids*), who explain faith and law to them from the tradition of the Sacred Family. The great majority of Mohammedans, as they do not accept this legitimist theory, are counted by the Shi'ah outside Arabia as unclean heretics, if not as unbelievers.

At the beginning of the fifteenth century this Shi'ah found its political centre in Persia, and opposed itself fanatically to the Sultan of Turkey, who at about the same time came to stand at the head of orthodox Islam. All differences of doctrine were now sharpened and embittered by political passion, and the efforts of single enlightened princes or scholars to induce the various peoples to extend to each other, across the political barriers, the hand of brotherhood in the principles of faith, all failed. It is only in the last few years that the general political distress of Islam has inclined the estranged relatives towards reconciliation.

Besides the veneration of the Alids, orthodox Islam has adopted another Shiitic element, the expectation of the Mahdi, which we have just mentioned. Most Sunnites expect that at the end of the world there will come from the House of Mohammed a successor to him, guided by Allah, who will maintain the revealed law as faithfully as the first four khalifs did according to the idealized history, and who will succeed with God's help in making Islam victorious over the whole world. That the chiliastic kingdom of the Mahdi must in the end be destroyed by Anti-Christ, in order that Jesus may be able once more to re-establish the holy order before the Resurrection, was a necessary consequence of the amalgamation of the political expectations formed under Shi'itic influence, with eschatological conceptions formerly borrowed by Islam from Christianity.

The orthodox Mahdi differs from that of the Shi'ah in many ways. He is not an *imam* returning after centuries of disappearance, but a descendant of Mohammed, coming into the world in the ordinary way to fulfill the ideal of the Khalifate. He does not re-establish the legitimate line of successors of the Prophet; but he renews the glorious tradition of the Khalifate, which after the first thirty years was dragged into the general deterioration, common to all human things. The prophecies concerning his appearance are sometimes of an equally supernatural kind as those of the Shiites, so that the period of his coming has passed more and more from the political sphere to which it originally belonged, into that of eschatology. Yet, naturally, it is easier for a popular leader to make himself regarded as the orthodox Mahdi than to play the part of the returned *imam*. Mohammedan rulers have had more trouble than they cared for with candidates for the dignity of the Mahdi; and it is not surprising that in official Turkish circles there is a tendency to simplify the Messianic expectation by giving the fullest weight to this traditional saying of Mohammed "There is no mahdi but Jesus," seeing that Jesus must come from the clouds, whereas other mahdis may arise from human society.

In the orthodox expectation of the Mahdi the Moslim theory has most sharply expressed its condemnation of the later political history of Islam. In the course of the first century after the Hijrah the Qoran scholars (*garis*) arose; and these in turn were succeeded by the men of tradition (ahl al-hadith) and by the canonists (*faqihs*) of later times. These learned men (ulama') would not endure any interference with their right to state with authority what Islam demanded of its leaders. They laid claim to an interpretative authority concerning the divine law, which bordered upon supreme legislative power; their agreement (Ijma') was that of the infallible community. But just as beside this legislative agreement, a dogmatic and a mystic agreement grew up, in the same way there was a separate Ijma' regarding the political government, upon which the canonists could exercise only an indirect influence. In other words since the accession of the Omayyad khalifs, the actual authority rested in the hands of dynasties, and under the Abbasids government assumed even a despotic character. This relation between the governors and governed, originally alien to Islam, was not changed by the transference of the actual power into the hands of *wezirs* and officers of the bodyguard; nor yet by the disintegration of the empire into a number of small despotisms, the investiture of which by the khalif became a mere formality. Dynastic and political questions were settled in a comparatively small circle, by court intrigue, stratagems, and force; and the canonists, like the people, were bound to accept the results. Politically inclined interpreters of the law might try to justify their compulsory assent to the facts by theories about the Ijma' of the notables residing in the capital, who took the urgent decisions about the succession, which decisions were subsequently confirmed by general homage to the new prince; but they had no illusions about the real influence of the community upon the choice of its leader. The most independent scholars made no attempt to disguise the fact that the course which political affairs had taken was the clearest proof of the moral degeneration which had set in, and they pronounced an equally bold and merciless criticism upon the government in all its departments. It became a matter of course that a pious scholar must keep himself free from all intercourse with state officials, on pain of losing his reputation.

The bridge across the gulf that separated the spiritual from the temporal authorities was formed by those state officials who, for the practice of their office, needed a knowledge of the divine law, especially the *qadhis*. It was originally the duty of these judges to decide all legal differences between Mohammedans, or men of other creeds under Mohammedan protection, who called for their decision. The actual division between the rulers and the interpreters of the law caused an ever-increasing limitation of the authority of the *qadhis*. The laws of marriage, family, and inheritance remained, however, their inalienable territory; and a number of other matters, in which too great a religious interest was involved to leave them to the caprice of the governors or to the customary law outside Islam, were usually included. But as the *qadhis* were appointed by the governors, they were obliged in the exercise of their office to give due consideration to the wishes of their constituents; and moreover they were often tainted by what was regarded in Mohammedan countries as inseparable from government employment: bribery.

On this account, the canonists, although it was from their ranks that the officials of the *qadhi* court were to be drawn, considered no words too strong to express their contempt for the office of *qadhi*. In handbooks of the Law of all times, the qadhis "of our time" are represented as unscrupulous beings, whose unreliable judgments were chiefly dictated by their greed. Such an opinion would not have acquired full force, if it had not been ascribed to Mohammed; in fact, the Prophet, according to a tradition, had said that out of three *qadhis* two are destined to Hell. Anecdotes of famous scholars who could not be prevailed upon by imprisonment or castigation to accept the office of *qadhis* are innumerable. Those who succumbed to the temptation forfeited the respect of the circle to which they had belonged.

I once witnessed a case of this kind, and the former friends of the *qadhi* did not spare him their bitter reproaches. He remarked that the judge, whose duty it was to maintain the divine law, verily held a noble office. They refuted this by saying that this defence was admissible only for earlier and better times, but not for "the *qadhis* of our time." To which he cuttingly replied "And ye, are ye canonists of the better, the ancient time?" In truth, the students of sacred science are just as much "of our time" as the *qadhis*. Even in the eleventh century the great theologian Ghazali counted them all equal.[17] Not a few of them give their authoritative advice according to the wishes of the highest bidder or of him who has the greatest influence, hustle for income from pious institutions, and vie with each other in a revel of casuistic subtleties. But among those scholars there are and always have been some who, in poverty and simplicity, devote their life to the study of Allah's law with the sole object of pleasing him; among the *qadhis* such are not easily to be found. Amongst the other state officials the title of *qadhi* may count as a spiritual one, and the public may to a certain extent share this reverence; but in the eyes of the pious and of the canonists such glory is only reflected from the clerical robe, in which the worldling disguises himself.

To the *mufti criticism is somewhat more favourable than to the qadhi*. A mufti is not necessarily an official; every canonist who, at the request of a layman, expounds to him the meaning of the law on any particular point and gives a *fatwa*, acts as a *mufti*. Be the question in reference to the behaviour of the individual towards God or towards man, with regard to his position in a matter of litigation, in criticism of a state regulation or of a sentence of a judge, or out of pure love of knowledge, the scholar is morally obliged to the best of his knowledge to enlighten the enquirer. He ought to do this for the love of God; but he must live, and the enquirer is expected to give him a suitable present for his trouble. This again gives rise to the danger that he who offers most is attended to first; and that for the liberal rich man a dish is prepared from the casuistic store, as far as possible according to his taste. The temptation is by no means so great as that to which the *qadhi* is exposed; especially since the office of judge has become an article of commerce, so that the very first step towards the possession of it is in the direction of Hell. Moreover in "these

---

17 Ghazali, *Ihya*, book i., ch. 6, quotes the words of a pious scholar of the olden time: "The 'ulama' will (on the Day of judgment) be gathered amongst the prophets, but the *qadhis* amongst the temporal rulers." Ghazali adds "alike with these *qadhis* are all those canonists who make use of their learning for worldly purposes."

degenerate times"—which have existed for about ten centuries—the acceptance of an appointment to the function of *qadhi* is not regarded as a duty, while a competent scholar may only refuse to give a *fatwa* under exceptional circumstances. Still, an unusually strong character is needed by the *mufti*, if he is not to fall into the snares of the world.

Besides *qadhis* who settle legal disputes of a certain kind according to the revealed law, the state requires its own advisers who can explain that law, i.e., official *muftis*. Firstly, the government itself may be involved in a litigation; moreover in some government regulations it may be necessary to avoid giving offence to canonists and their strict disciples. In such cases it is better to be armed beforehand with an expert opinion than to be exposed to dangerous criticism which might find an echo in a wide circle. The official *mufti* must therefore be somewhat pliable, to say the least. Moreover, any private person has the right to put questions to the state *mufti*; and the *qadhi* court is bound to take his answers into account in its decisions. In this way the *muftis have absorbed a part of the duties of the qadhis*, and so their office is dragged along in the degradation that the unofficial canonists denounce unweariedly in their writings and in their teaching.

The way in which the most important *mufti* places are filled and above all the position which the head-*mufti* of the Turkish Empire, the Sheikh-ul-Islam, holds at any particular period, may well serve as a touchstone of the influence of the canonists on public life. If this is great, then even the most powerful sultan has only the possibility of choice between a few great scholars, put forward or at all events not disapproved of by their own guild, strengthened by public opinion. If, on the other hand, there is no keen interest felt in the Shari'ah (Divine Law), then the temporal rulers can do pretty much what they like with these representatives of the canon law. Under the tyrannical sway of Sultan Abd-ul-Hamid, the Sheikh-ul-Islam was little more than a tool for him and his palace clique, and for their own reasons, the members of the Committee of Union and Progress, who rule at Constantinople since 1908, made no change in this: each new ministry had its own Sheikh-ul-Islam, who had to be, above everything, a faithful upholder of the constitutional theory held by the Committee. The time is past when the Sultan and the Porte, in framing even the most pressing reform, must first anxiously assure themselves of the position that the hojas, tolbas, softas, the theologians in a word, would take towards it, and of the influence that the Sheikh-ul-Islam could use in opposition to their plans. The political authority makes its deference to the canonists dependent upon their strict obedience.

This important change is a natural consequence of the modernization of Mohammedan political life, a movement through which the expounders of a law which has endeavoured to remain stationary since the year 1000 must necessarily get into straits. This explains also why the religious life of Mohammedans is in some respects freer in countries under non-Mohammedan authority, than under a Mohammedan government. Under English, Dutch, or French rule the 'ulamas are less interfered with in their teaching, the *muftis* in their recommendations, and the *qadhis* in their judgments of questions of marriage and inheritance than in Turkey, where the life of Islam, as state religion, lies under official control. In indirectly governed "native states" the relation of Mohammedan "Church and State" may much more resemble that in Turkey, and this is sometimes to the advantage of the sovereign ruler. Under the direct government of a modern state, the Mohammedan group is treated as a religious community, whose particular life has just the same claim to independence as that of other denominations. The only justifiable limitation is that the program of the forcible reduction of the world to Mohammedan authority be kept within the scholastic walls as a point of eschatology, and not considered as a body of prescriptions, the execution of which must be prepared.

The extensive political program of Islam, developed during the first centuries of astounding expansion, has yet not prevented millions of Mohammedans from resigning themselves to reversed conditions in which at the present time many more Mohammedans live under foreign authority than under their own. The acceptance of this change was facilitated by the historical pessimism of Islam, which makes the mind prepared for every sort of decay, and by the true Moslim habit of resignation to painful experiences, not through fatalism, but through reverence for Allah's inscrutable will. At the same time, it would be a gross mistake to imagine that the idea of universal conquest may be considered as obliterated. This is the case with the intellectuals and with many practical commercial or industrial men; but the canonists and the vulgar still live in the illusion of the days of Islam's greatness.

The legists continue to ground their appreciation of every actual political condition on the law of the holy war, which war ought never to be allowed to cease entirely until all mankind is reduced to the authority of Islam—the heathen by conversion, the adherents of acknowledged Scripture by submission. Even if they admit the improbability of this at present, they are comforted and encouraged by the recollection of the lengthy period of humiliation that the Prophet himself had to suffer before Allah bestowed victory upon his arms; and they fervently join with the Friday preacher, when he pronounces the prayer, taken from the Qoran: "And lay not on us, O our Lord, that for which we have not strength, but blot out our sins and forgive us and have pity upon us. Thou art our Master; grant us then to conquer the unbelievers!" And the common people are willingly taught by the canonists and feed their hope of better days upon the innumerable legends of the olden time and the equally innumerable apocalyptic prophecies about the future. The political blows that fall upon Islam make less impression upon their simple minds than the senseless stories about the power of the Sultan of Stambul, that would instantly be revealed if he were not surrounded by treacherous servants, and the fantastic tidings of the miracles that Allah works in the Holy Cities of Arabia which are inaccessible to the unfaithful.

The conception of the Khalifate still exercises a fascinating influence, regarded in the light of a central point of union against the unfaithful. Apart from the 'amils, Mohammed's agents amongst the Arabian tribes, the Khalifate was the only political institution which arose out of the necessity of the Moslim community, without foreign influence. It rescued Islam from threatening destruction, and it led the Faithful to conquest. No wonder that in historic legend the first four occupiers of that leadership, who, from Medina, accomplished such great things, have been glorified into saints, and are held up to all the following generations as examples to put them to shame. In the Omayyads the ancient aristocracy of Mecca came to the helm, and under them, the Mohammedan state was above all, as Wellhausen styled it, "the Arabian Empire." The best khalifs of this house had the political wisdom to give the governors of the provinces sufficient independence to prevent schism, and to secure to themselves the authority in important matters. The reaction of the non-Arabian converts against the suppression of their own culture by the Arabian conquerors found support in the opposition parties, above all with the Shi'ah. The Abbasids, cleverer politicians than the notoriously unskillful Alids, made use of the Alid propaganda to secure the booty to themselves at the right moment. The means which served the Alids for the establishment only of an invisible dynasty of princes who died as martyrs, enabled the descendants of Mohammed's uncle Abbas to overthrow the Omayyads, and to found their own Khalifate at Bagdad, shining with the brilliance of an Eastern despotism.

When it is said that the Abbasid Khalifate maintained itself from 750 till the Mongol storm in the middle of the thirteenth century, that only refers to external appearance. After a brief success, the actual power of these khalifs was transferred to the hands, first, of the captains of their bodyguard, then of sultan-dynasties, whose forcibly acquired powers, were legalized by a formal investiture. In the same way the large provinces developed into independent kingdoms, whose rulers considered the nomination-diplomas from Bagdad in the light of mere ornaments. Compared to this irreparable disintegration of the empire, temporary schisms such as the Omayyad Khalifate in Spain, the Fatimid Khalifate in Egypt, and here and there an independent organization of the Kharijites were of little significance.

It seems strange that the Moslim peoples, although the theory of Islam never attributed an hereditary character to the Khalifate, attached so high a value to the Abbasid name, that they continued unanimously to acknowledge the Khalifate of Bagdad for centuries during which it possessed no influence. But the idea of hereditary rulers was deeply rooted in most of the peoples converted to Islam, and the glorious period of the first Abbasids so strongly impressed itself on the mind of the vulgar, that the *appearance of continuation was easily taken for reality*. Its voidness would sooner have been realized, if lack of energy had not prevented the later Abbasids from trying to recover the lost power by the sword, or if amongst their rivals who could also boast of a popular tradition—e.g., the Omayyads, or still more the Alids—a political genius had succeeded in forming a powerful opposition. But the sultans who ruled the various states did not want to place all that they possessed in the balance on the chance of gaining the title of Khalif. The Moslim world became accustomed to the idea that the honoured House of the Prophet's uncle Abbas existed for the purpose of lending an additional glory to Mohammedan princes by a diploma. Even after the destruction of Bagdad by the Mongols in 1258, from which only a few Abbasids escaped alive, Indian princes continued to value visits or deeds of appointment granted them by some begging descendant of the "Glorious House." The sultans of Egypt secured this luxury permanently for themselves by taking a branch of the family under their protection, who gave the glamour of their approval to every new result of the never-ending quarrels of succession, until in the beginning of the sixteenth century Egypt, together with so many other lands, was swallowed up by the Turkish conqueror.

These new rulers, who added the Byzantine Empire to Islam, who with Egypt brought Southern and Western Arabia with the Holy Cities also under their authority, and caused all the neighbouring princes, Moslim and Christian alike, to tremble on their thrones, thought it was time to abolish the senseless survival of the Abbasid glory. The prestige of the Ottomans was as great as that of the Khalifate in its most palmy days had been; and they would not be withheld from the assumption of the title. There is a doubtful tale of the abdication of the Abbasids in their favour, but the question is of no importance. The Ottomans owed their Khalifate to their sword; and this was the only argument used by such canonists as thought it worth their while to bring such an incontestable fact into reconciliation with the law. This was not strictly necessary, as they had been accustomed for eight centuries to acquiesce in all sorts of unlawful acts which history demonstrated to be the will of Allah.

The sense of the tradition that established descent from the tribe of Qoraish as necessary for the highest dignity in the community was capable of being weakened by explanation; and, even without that, the leadership of the irresistible Ottomans was of more value to Islam than the chimerical authority of a powerless Qoraishite. In our own time, you can hear Qoraishites, and even Alids, warmly defend the claims of the Turkish sultans to the Khalifate, as they regard these as the only Moslim princes capable of championing the threatened rights of Islam.

Even the sultans of Stambul could not think of restoring the authority of the Khalif over the whole Mohammedan world. This was prevented not only by the schismatic kingdoms, khalifates, or imamates like Shi'itic Persia, which was consolidated just in the sixteenth century, by the unceasing opposition of the Imams of Yemen, and Kharijite principalities at the extremities of the Mohammedan world. Besides these, there were numerous princes in Central Asia, in India, and in Central Africa, whom either the Khalifate had always been obliged to leave to themselves, or who had become so estranged from it that, unless they felt the power of the Turkish arms, they preferred to remain as they were. Moreover, Islam had extended itself not only by political means, but also by trade and colonization into countries even the existence of which was hardly known in the political centres of Islam, e.g., into Central Africa or the Far East of Asia. Without thinking of rivalling the Abbasids or their successors, some of the princes of such remote kingdoms, e.g., the sherifs of Morocco, assumed the title of Commander of the Faithful, bestowed upon them by their flatterers. Today, there are petty princes in East India under Dutch sovereignty who decorate themselves with the title of Khalif, without suspecting that they are thereby guilty of a sort of arrogant blasphemy.

Such exaggeration is not supported by the canonists; but these have devised a theory, which gives a foundation to the authority of Mohammedan princes, who never had a real or fictitious connection with a real or fictitious Khalifate. Authority there must be, everywhere and under all circumstances; far from the centre this should be exercised, according to them, by the one who has been able to gain it and who knows how to hold it; and all the duties are laid upon him, which, in a normal condition, would be discharged by the Khalif or his representative. For this kind of authority the legists have even invented a special name: "*shaukah,*" which means actual influence, the authority which has spontaneously arisen in default of a chief who in one form or another can be considered as a mandatary of the Khalifate.

Now, it is significant that many of those Mohammedan governors, who owe their existence to wild growth in this way, seek, especially in our day, for connection with the Khalifate, or, at least, wish to be regarded as naturally connected with the centre. The same is true of such whose former independence or adhesion to the Turkish Empire has been replaced by the sovereignty of a Western state. Even amongst the Moslim peoples placed under the direct government of European states a tendency prevails to be considered in some way or another subjects of the Sultan-Khalif. Some scholars explain this phenomenon by the spiritual character which the dignity of Khalif is supposed to have acquired under the later Abbasids, and retained since that time, until the Ottoman princes combined it again with the temporal dignity of sultan. According to this view the later Abbasids were a sort of popes of Islam; while the temporal authority, in the central districts as well as in the subordinate kingdoms, was in the hands of various sultans. The sultans of Constantinople govern, then, under this name, as much territory as the political vicissitudes allow them to govern — *i.e.*, the Turkish Empire; as khalifs, they are the spiritual heads of the whole of Sunnite Islam.

Though this view, through the ignorance of European statesmen and diplomatists, may have found acceptance even by some of the great powers, it is nevertheless entirely untrue; unless by "spiritual authority" we are to understand the empty appearance of worldly authority. This appearance was all that the later Abbasids retained after the loss of their temporal power; spiritual authority of any kind they never possessed.

The spiritual authority in catholic Islam reposes in the legists, who in this respect are called in a tradition the "heirs of the prophets." Since they could no longer regard the khalifs as their leaders, because they walked in worldly ways, they have constituted themselves independently beside and even above them; and the rulers have been obliged to conclude a silent contract with them, each party binding itself to remain within its own limits.[18] If this contract be observed, the legists not only are ready to acknowledge the bad rulers of the world, but even to preach loyalty towards them to the laity.

The most supremely popular part of the ideal of Islam, the reduction of the whole world to Moslim authority, can only be attempted by a political power. Notwithstanding the destructive criticism of all Moslim princes and state officials by the canonists, it was only from them that they could expect measures to uphold and extend the power of Islam; and on this account they continually cherished the ideal of the Khalifate.

In the first centuries it was the duty of Mohammedans who had become isolated, and who had for instance been conquered by "unbelievers," to do "hijrah," i.e., emigration for Allah's sake, as the converted Arabs had done in Mohammed's time by emigrating to Medina to strengthen the ranks of the Faithful. This soon became impracticable, so that the legists relaxed the prescription by concessions to "the force of necessity." Resignation was thus permitted, even recommended;

---

18   That the Khalifate is in no way to be compared with the Papacy, that Islam has never regarded the Khalif as its spiritual head, I have repeatedly explained since 1882 (in "Nieuwe Bijdragen tot de kennis van den Islam," in Bijdr. tot de Taal, Landen Volkenkunde van Nederl. Indie, Volgr. 4, Deel vi, in an article, "De Islam," in *De Gids*, May, 1886, in *Questions Diplomatiques et Coloniales*, 5me annee, No. 106, etc.). I am pleased to find the same views expressed by Prof. M. Hartmann in *Die Welt des Islams*, Bd. i., pp. 147-8.

but the submission to non-Musulmans was always to be regarded as temporary and abnormal. Although the *partes infidelium* have grown larger and larger, the eye must be kept fixed upon the centre, the Khalifate, where every movement towards improvement must begin. A Western state that admits any authority of a khalif over its Mohammedan subjects, thus acknowledges, *not* the authority of a pope of the Moslim Church, but in simple ignorance is feeding political programs, which, however vain, always have the power of stirring Mohammedan masses to confusion and excitement.

Of late years Mohammedan statesmen in their intercourse with their Western colleagues are glad to take the latter's point of view; and, in discussion, accept the comparison of the Khalifate with the Papacy, because they are aware that only in this form the Khalifate can be made acceptable to powers who have Mohammedan subjects. But for these subjects the Khalif is then their true prince, who is temporarily hindered in the exercise of his government, but whose right is acknowledged even by their unbelieving masters.

In yet another respect the canonists need the aid of the temporal rulers. An alert police is counted by them amongst the indispensable means of securing purity of doctrine and life. They count it to the credit of princes and governors that they enforced by violent measures seclusion and veiling of the women, abstinence from drinking, and that they punished by flogging the negligent with regard to fasting or attending public worship. The political decay of Islam, the increasing number of Mohammedans under foreign rule, appears to them, therefore, doubly dangerous, as they have little faith in the proof of Islam's spiritual goods against life in a freedom which to them means license.

They find that every political change, in these terrible times, is to the prejudice of Islam, one Moslim people after another losing its independent existence; and they regard it as equally dangerous that Moslim princes are induced to accommodate their policy and government to new international ideas of individual freedom, which threaten the very life of Islam. They see the antagonism to all foreign ideas, formerly considered as a virtue by every true Moslim, daily losing ground, and they are filled with consternation by observing in their own ranks the contamination of modernist ideas. The brilliant development of the system of Islam followed the establishment of its material power; so the rapid decline of that political power which we are witnessing makes the question urgent, whether Islam has a spiritual essence able to survive the fall of such a material support. It is certainly not the canonists who will detect the kernel; "verily we are God's and verily to Him do we return," they cry in helpless amazement, and their consolation is in the old prayer: "And lay not on us, O our Lord, that for which we have no strength, but blot out our sins and forgive us and have mercy upon us. Thou art our Master; grant us then to conquer the Unbelievers!"

IV

Islam And Modern Thought

ONE of the most powerful factors of religious life in its higher forms is the need of man to find in this world of changing things an imperishable essence, to separate the eternal from the temporal and then to attach himself to the former. Where the possibility of this operation is despaired of, there may arise a pessimism, which finds no path of liberation from the painful vicissitudes of life other than the annihilation of individuality. A firm belief in a sphere of life freed from the category of time, together with the conviction that the poetic images of that superior world current among mankind are images and nothing else, is likely to give rise to definitions of the Absolute by purely negative attributes and to mental efforts having for their object the absorption of individual existence in the indescribable infinite. Generally speaking, a high development of intellectual life, especially an intimate acquaintance with different religious systems, is not favourable to the continuance of elaborate conceptions of things eternal; it will rather increase the tendency to deprive the idea of the Transcendent of all colour and definiteness.

The naive ideas concerning the other world in the clear-cut form outlined for them by previous generations are most likely to remain unchanged in a religious community where intellectual intercourse is chiefly limited to that between members of the community. There the belief is fostered that things most appreciated and cherished in this fading world by mankind will have an enduring existence in a world to come, and that the best of the changing phenomena of life are eternal and will continue free from that change, which is the principal cause of human misery. Material death will be followed by awakening to a purer life, the idealized continuation of life on earth, and for this reason already during this life the faithful will find their delight in those things which they know to be everlasting.

The less faith is submitted to the control of intellect, the more numerous the objects will be to which durable value is attributed. This is true for different individuals as well as for one religious community as compared to another. There are Christians attached only to the spirit of the Gospel, Mohammedans attached only to the spirit of the Qoran. Others give a place in their world of imperishable things to a particular translation of the Bible in its old-fashioned orthography or to a written Qoran in preference to a printed one. Orthodox Judaism and orthodox Islam have marked with the stamp of eternity codes of law, whose influence has worked as an impediment to the life of the adherents of those religions and to the free intercourse of other people with them as well. So the Roman Catholic and many Protestant Churches have in their organizations and in their dogmatic systems eternalized institutions and ideas whose unchangeableness has come to retard spiritual progress.

Among all conservative factors of human life religion must necessarily be the most conservative, were it only because its aim is precisely to store up and keep under its guardianship the treasures destined for eternity to which we have alluded. Now, every new period in the history of civilization obliges a religious community to undertake a general revision of the contents of its treasury. It is unavoidable that the guardians on such occasions should be in a certain measure disappointed, for they find that some of, the goods under their care have given way to the wasting influence of time, whilst others are in a state which gives rise to serious doubt as to their right of being classified with lasting treasures. In reality the loss is only an apparent one; far from impoverishing the community, it enhances the solidity of its possessions. What remains after the sifting process may be less imposing to the inexperienced mind; gradually the consideration gains ground that what has been rejected was nothing but useless rubbish which had been wrongly valued.

Sometimes it may happen that the general movement of spiritual progress goes almost too fast, so that one revision of the stores of religion is immediately followed by another. Then dissension is likely to arise among the adherents of a religion;

some of them come to the conclusion that there must be an end of sifting and think it better to lock up the treasuries once for all and to stop the dangerous enquiries; whereas others begin to entertain doubt concerning the value even of such goods as do not yet show any trace of decay.

The treasuries of Islam are excessively full of rubbish that has become entirely useless; and for nine or ten centuries they have not been submitted to a revision deserving that name. If we wish to understand the whole or any important part of the system of Islam, we must always begin by transporting ourselves into the third or fourth century of the Hijrah, and we must constantly bear in mind that from the Medina period downwards Islam has always been considered by its adherents as bound to regulate all the details of their life by means of prescriptions emanating directly or indirectly from God, and therefore incapable of being reformed. At the time when these prescriptions acquired their definite form, Islam ruled an important portion of the world; it considered the conquest of the rest as being only a question of time; and, therefore, felt itself quite independent in the development of its law. There was little reason indeed for the Moslim canonists to take into serious account the interests of men not subject to Mohammedan authority or to care for the opinion of devotees of other religions. Islam might act, and did almost act, as if it were the only power in the world; it did so in the way of a grand seigneur, showing a great amount of generosity towards its subjugated enemies. The adherents of other religions were or would become subjects of the Commander of the Faithful; those subjects were given a full claim on Mohammedan protection and justice; while the independent unbelievers were in general to be treated as enemies until in submission. Their spiritual life deserved not even so much attention as that of Islam received from Abbe Maracci or Doctor Prideaux. The false doctrines of other peoples were of no interest whatever in themselves; and, since there was no fear of Mohammedans being tainted by them, polemics against the abrogated religions were more of a pastime than an indispensable part of theology. The Mohammedan community being in a sense Allah's army, with the conquest of the world as its object, apostasy deserved the punishment of death in no lesser degree than desertion in the holy war, nay more so; for the latter might be the effect of cowardice, whereas the former was an act of inexcusable treachery.

In the attitude of Islam towards other religions there is hardly one feature that has not its counterpart in the practice of Christian states during the Middle Ages. The great difference is that the Mohammedan community erected this medieval custom into a system unalterable like all prescriptions based on its infallible "Agreement" (Ijma'). Here lay the great difficulty when the nineteenth and twentieth centuries placed the Moslim world face to face with a civilization that had sprung up outside its borders and without its collaboration, that was from a spiritual point of view by far its superior and at the same time possessed of sufficient material power to thrust the Mohammedans aside wherever they seemed to be an impediment in its way. A long series of the most painful experiences, meaning as many encroachments upon the political independence of Mohammedan territories, ended by teaching Islam that it had definitely to change its lines of conduct. The times were gone when relations with the non-Musulman world quite different from those foreseen by the mediaeval theory might be considered as exceptions to the rule, as temporary concessions to transitory necessities. In ever wider circles a thorough revision of the system came to be considered as a requirement of the time. The fact that the number of Mohammedans subject to foreign rule increased enormously, and by far surpassed those of the citizens of independent Mohammedan states, made the problem almost as interesting to Western nations as to the Mohammedans themselves. Both parties are almost equally concerned in the question, whether a way will be found to associate the Moslim world to modern civilization, without obliging it to empty its spiritual treasury altogether. Nobody can in earnest advocate the idea of leaving the solution of the problem to rude force. The Moslim of yore, going through the world with the Qoran in one hand, the sword in the other, giving unbelievers the choice between conversion or death, is a creation of legendary fancy. We can but hope that modern civilization will not be so fanatical against Moslims, as the latter were unjustly said to have been during the period of their power. If the modern world were only to offer the Mohammedans the choice between giving up at once the traditions of their ancestors or being treated as barbarians, there would be sure to ensue a struggle as bloody as has ever been witnessed in the world. It is worth while indeed to examine the system of Islam from this special point of view, and to try to find the terms on which a durable *modus vivendi* might be established between Islam and modern thought.

The purely dogmatic part is not of great importance. Some of us may admire the tenets of the Mohammedan doctrine, others may as heartily despise them; to the participation of Mohammedans in the civilized life of our days they are as innoxious as any other mediaeval dogmatic system that counts its millions of adherents among ourselves. The details of Mohammedan dogmatics have long ceased to interest other circles than those of professional theologians; the chief points arouse no discussion and the deviations in popular superstition as well as in philosophical thought which in practice meet with toleration are almost unlimited. The Mohammedan Hell claims the souls of all heterodox people, it is true; but this does not prevent benevolent intercourse in this world, and more enlightened Moslims are inclined to enlarge their definition of the word "faithful" so as to include their non-Mohammedan friends. The faith in a Mahdi, who will come to regenerate the world, is apt to give rise to revolutionary movements led by skilful demagogues pretending to act as the "Guided One," or, at least, to prepare the way for his coming. Most of the European powers having Mohammedan subjects have had their disagreeable experiences in this respect. But Moslim chiefs of states have their obvious good reasons for not liking such movements either; and even the majority of ordinary Moslims look upon candidates for Mahdi-ship with suspicion. A contented prosperous population offers such candidates little chance of success.

The ritual laws of Islam are a heavy burden to those who strictly observe them; a man who has to perform worship five times a day in a state of ritual purity and during a whole month in a year has to abstain from food and drink and other enjoyments from daybreak until sunset, is at a disadvantage when he has to enter into competition with non-Musulmans for getting work of any kind. But since most of the Moslims have become subjects of foreign powers and religious police has been practically abolished in Mohammedan states, there is no external compulsion. The ever smaller minority of strict practisers make use of a right which nobody can contest.

Drinking wine or other intoxicating drinks, taking interest on money, gambling—including even insurance contracts according to the stricter interpretation—are things which a Moslim may abstain from without hindering non-Mohammedans; or which in our days he may do, notwithstanding the prohibition of divine law, even without losing his good name.

Those who want to accentuate the antithesis between Islam and modern civilization point rightly to the personal law; here is indeed a great stumbling-block. The allowance of polygamy up to a maximum of four wives is represented by Mohammedan authors as a progress if compared with the irregularity of pagan Arabia and even with the acknowledgment of unlimited polygamy during certain periods of Biblical history. The following subtle argument is to be found in some schoolbooks on Mohammedan law: The law of Moses was exceedingly benevolent to males by permitting them to have an unlimited number of wives; then came the law of Jesus, extreme on the other side by prescribing monogamy; at last Mohammed restored the equilibrium by conceding one wife to each of the four humours which make up the male's constitution. This theory, which leaves the question what the woman is to do with three of her four humours undecided, will hardly find fervent advocates among the present canonists. At the same time, very few of them would venture to pronounce their preference for monogamy in a general way, polygamy forming a part of the law that is to prevail, according to the infallible Agreement of the Community, until the Day of Resurrection.

On the other side polygamy, although *allowed*, is far from being *recommended* by the majority of theologians. Many of them even dissuade men capable of mastering their passion from marriage in general, and censure a man who takes two wives if he can live honestly with one. In some Mohammedan countries social circumstances enforce practical monogamy. The whole question lies in the education of women; when this has been raised to a higher level, polygamy will necessarily come to an end. It is therefore most satisfactory that among male Mohammedans the persuasion of the necessity of a solid education for girls is daily gaining ground. This year (1913), a young Egyptian took his doctor's degree at the Paris University by sustaining a dissertation on the position of women in the Moslim world, in which he told his co-religionists the full truth concerning this rather delicate subject[19]. If social evolution takes the right course, the practice of polygamy will be abolished; and the maintenance of its lawfulness in canonical works will mainly be a survival of a bygone phase of development.

---

19   Mansour Fahmy, La condition de la femme dans la tradition et l'evolution de l'Islamisme, Paris, Felix Alcan, 1913. The sometimes imprudent form in which the young reformer enounced his ideas caused him to be very badly treated by his compatriots at his return from Europe.

The facility with which a man can divorce his wife at his pleasure, contrasted with her rights against him, is a still more serious impediment to the development of family life than the institution of polygamy; more serious, also, than veiling and seclusion of women. Where the general opinion is favourable to the improvement of the position of women in society, there is always found a way to secure it to them without conflicting with the divine law; but a radical reform will remain most difficult so long as that law which allows the man to repudiate his wife without any reason, whereas it delivers the woman almost unarmed into the power of her husband, is considered to be one of the permanent treasures of Islam.

It is a pity indeed that thus far women vigorously striving for liberation from those mediaeval institutions are rare exceptions in Mohammedan countries. Were Mohammedan women capable of the violent tactics of suffragettes, they would rather try to blow up the houses of feminists than those of the patrons of the old regime. The ordinary Mohammedan woman looks upon the endeavour of her husband to induce her to partake freely in public life as a want of consideration; it makes on her about the same impression as that which a respectable woman in our society would receive from her husband encouraging her to visit places generally frequented by people of bad reputation. It is the girls' school that will awaken those sleeping ones and so, slowly and gradually, prepare a better future, when the Moslim woman will be the worthy companion of her husband and the intelligent educator of her children. This will be due, then, neither to the Prophet's Sunnah nor to the infallible Agreement of the Community of the first centuries of Islam, but to the irresistible power of the evolution of human society, which is merciless to laws even of divine origin and transfers them, when their time is come, from the treasury of everlasting goods to a museum of antiquities.

Slavery, and in its consequence free intercourse of a man with his own female slaves without any limitation as to their number, has also been incorporated into the sacred law, and therefore has been placed on the wrong side of the border that is to divide eternal things from temporal ones. This should not be called a mediaeval institution; the most civilized nations not having given it up before the middle of the nineteenth century. The law of Islam regulated the position of slaves with much equity, and there is a great body of testimony from people who have spent a part of their lives among Mohammedan nations which does justice to the benevolent treatment which bondmen generally receive from their masters there. Besides that, we are bound to state that in many Western countries or countries under Western domination whole groups of the population live under circumstances with which those of Mohammedan slavery may be compared to advantage.

The only legal cause of slavery in Islam is prisonership of war or birth from slave parents. The captivity of enemies of Islam has not at all necessarily the effect of enslaving them; for the competent authorities may dispose of them in any other way, also in the way prescribed by modern international law or custom. In proportion to the realization of the political ideal of Islam the number of its enemies must diminish and the possibilities of enslaving men must consequently decrease. Setting slaves free is one of the most meritorious pious works, and, at the same time, the regular atonement for certain transgressions of the sacred law. So, according to Mohammedan principles, slavery is an institution destined to disappear. When, in the last century, Mohammedan princes signed international treaties for the suppression of slavery, from their point of view this was a premature anticipation of a future political and social development—a step which they felt obliged to take out of consideration for the great powers. In Arabia, every effort of the Turkish Government to put such international agreements into execution has thus far given rise to popular sedition against the Ottoman authority. Therefore, the promulgation of decrees of abolition was stopped; and slavery continued to exist. The import of slaves from Africa has, in fact, considerably diminished; but I am not quite sure of the proportional increase of the liberty which the natives of that continent enjoy at home.

Slavery as well as polygamy is in a certain sense to Mohammedans a sacred institution, being incorporated in their Holy Law; but the practice of neither of the two institutions is indispensable to the integrity of Islam.

All those antiquated institutions, if considered from the point of view of modern international intercourse, are only a trifle in comparison with the legal prescriptions of Islam concerning the attitude of the Mohammedan community against the parts of the world not yet subject to its authority, "the Abode of War" as they are technically called. It is a principal duty of the Khalif, or of the chiefs considered as his substitutes in different countries, to avail themselves of every opportunity to extend by force the dominion of Allah and His Messenger. With unsubdued unbelievers *peace is not allowed*; a *truce* for a period not exceeding ten years may be concluded if the interest of Islam requires it.

The chapters of the Mohammedan law on holy war and on the conditions on which the submission of the adherents of tolerated religions is to be accepted seem to be a foolish pretension if we consider them by the light of the actual division of political power in the world. But here, too, to understand is better than to ridicule. In the centuries in which the system of Islam acquired its maturity, such an aspiration after universal dominion was not at all ridiculous; and many Christian states of the time were far from reaching the Mohammedan standard of tolerance against heterodox creeds. The delicate point is this, that the petrification or at least the process of stiffening that has attacked the whole spiritual life of Islam since about 1000 A.D. makes its accommodation to the requirements of modern intercourse a most difficult problem.

But it is not only the Mohammedan community that needed misfortune and humiliation before it was able to appreciate liberty of conscience; or that took a long time to digest those painful lessons of history. There are still Christian Churches which accept religious liberty only in circumstances that make supreme authority unattainable to them; and which, elsewhere, would not disdain the use of material means to subdue spirits to what they consider the absolute truth.

To judge such things with equity, we must remember that every man possessed of a firm conviction of any kind is more or less a missionary; and the belief in the possibility of winning souls by violence has many adherents everywhere. One of my friends among the young-Turkish state officials, who wished to persuade me of the perfect religious tolerance of Turkey of today, concluded his argument by the following reflection: "Formerly men used to behead each other for difference of opinion about the Hereafter. Nowadays, praise be to Allah, we are permitted to believe what we like; but people continue to kill each other for political or social dissension. That is most pitiful indeed; for the weapons in use being more terrible and more costly than before, mankind lacks the peace necessary to enjoy the liberty of conscience it has acquired."

The truthful irony of these words need not prevent us from considering the independence of spiritual life and the liberation of its development from material compulsion as one of the greatest blessings of our civilization. We feel urged by missionary zeal of the better kind to make the Mohammedan world partake in its enjoyment. In the Turkish Empire, in Egypt, in many Mohammedan countries under Western control, the progressive elements of Moslim society spontaneously meet us half-way. But behind them are the millions who firmly adhere to the old superstition and are supported by the canonists, those faithful guardians of what the infallible Community declared almost one thousand years ago to be the doctrine and rule of life for all centuries to come. Will it ever prove possible to move in one direction a body composed of such different elements, or will this body be torn in pieces when the movement has become irresistible?

We have more than once pointed to the catholic character of orthodox Islam. In fact, the diversity of spiritual tendencies is not less in the Moslim world than within the sphere of Christian influence; but in Islam, apart from the political schisms of the first centuries, that diversity has not given rise to anything like the division of Christianity into sects. There is a prophetic saying, related by Tradition, which later generations have generally misunderstood to mean that the Mohammedan community would be split into seventy-three different sects. Moslim heresiologists have been induced by this prediction to fill up their lists of seventy-three numbers with all sorts of names, many of which represent nothing but individual opinions of more or less famous scholars on subordinate points of doctrine or law. Almost ninety-five per cent. of all Mohammedans are indeed bound together by a spiritual unity that may be compared with that of the Roman Catholic Church, within whose walls there is also room for religious and intellectual life of very different origin and tendency. In the sense of broadness, Islam has this advantage, that there is no generally recognized palpable authority able to stop now and then the progress of modernism or similar deviations from the trodden path with an imperative "Halt!" There is no lack indeed of mutual accusation of heresy; but this remains without serious consequences because of the absence of a high ecclesiastical council competent to decide once for all. The political authorities, who might be induced by fanatical theologians to settle disputes by violent inquisitorial means, have been prevented for a long time from such interference by more pressing affairs.

A knowledge alone of the orthodox system of Islam, however complete, would give us an even more inadequate idea of the actual world of catholic Islam than the notion we should acquire of the spiritual currents moving the Roman Catholic world by merely studying the dogma and the canonical law of the Church of Rome.

Nevertheless, the unity of Islamic thought is by no means a word void of sense. The ideas of Mohammedan philosophers, borrowed for a great part from Neoplatonism, the pantheism and the emanation theory of Mohammedan mystics are certainly still further distant from the simplicity of Qoranic religion than the orthodox dogmatics; but all those conceptions alike show indubitable marks of having grown up on Mohammedan soil. In the works even of those mystics who efface the limits between things human and divine, who put Judaism, Christianity, and Paganism on the same line with the revelation of Mohammed, and who are therefore duly anathematized by the whole orthodox world, almost every page testifies to the relation of the ideas enounced with Mohammedan civilization. Most of the treatises on science, arts, or law written by Egyptian students for their doctor's degree at European universities make no exception to this rule; the manner in which these authors conceive the problems and strive for their solution is, in a certain sense, in the broadest sense of course, Mohammedan. Thus, if we speak of Mohammedan thought, civilization, spirit, we have to bear in mind the great importance of the system which, almost unchanged, has been delivered for about one thousand years by one generation of doctors of Islam to the other, although it has become ever more unfit to meet the needs of the Community, on whose infallible Agreement it rests. But, at the same time, we ought to consider that beside the agreement of canonists, of dogmatists, and of mystics, there are a dozen more agreements, social, political, popular, philosophical, and so on, and that however great may be the influence of the doctors, who pretend to monopolize infallibility for the opinions on which they agree, the real Agreement of Islam is the least common measure of all the agreements of the groups which make up the Community.

It would require a large volume to review the principal currents of thought pervading the Moslim world in our day; but a general notion may be acquired by a rapid glance at two centres, geographically not far distant from each other, but situated at the opposite poles of spiritual life: Mecca and Cairo.

In Mecca yearly two or three hundred thousand Moslims from all parts of the world come together to celebrate the hajj, that curious set of ceremonies of pagan Arabian origin which Mohammed has incorporated into his religion, a durable survival that in Islam makes an impression as singular as that of jumping processions in Christianity. Mohammed never could have foreseen that the consequence of his concession to deeply rooted Arabic custom would be that in future centuries Chinese, Malays, Indians, Tatars, Turks, Egyptians, Berbers, and negroes would meet on this barren desert soil and carry home profound impressions of the international significance of Islam. Still more important is the fact that from all those countries young people settle here for years to devote themselves to the study of the sacred science. From the second to the tenth month of the Mohammedan lunar year, the Haram, *i.e.*, the mosque, which is an open place with the Ka'bah in its midst and surrounded by large roofed galleries, has free room enough between the hours of public service to allow of a dozen or more circles of students sitting down around their professors to listen to as many lectures on different subjects, generally delivered in a very loud voice. Arabic grammar and style, prosody, logic, and other preparatory branches, the sacred trivium; canonic law, dogmatics, and mysticism, and, for the more advanced, exegesis of Qoran and Tradition and some other branches of supererogation, are taught here in the mediaeval way from mediaeval text-books or from more modern compilations reproducing their contents and completing them more or less by treating modern questions according to the same methods.

It is now almost thirty years since I lived the life of a Meccan student during one university year, after having become familiar with the matter taught by the professors of the temple of Mecca, the Haram, by privately studying it, so that I could freely use all my time in observing the mentality of people learning those things not for curiosity, but in order to acquire the only true direction for their life in this world and the salvation of their souls in the world to come. For a modern man there could hardly be a better opportunity imagined for getting a true vision of the Middle Ages than is offered to the Orientalist by a few months' stay in the Holy City of Islam. In countries like China, Tibet, or India there are spheres of spiritual life which present to us still more interesting material for comparative study of religions than that of Mecca, because they are so much more distant from our own; but, just on that account, the Western student would not be able to adapt his mind to their mental atmospheres as he may do in Mecca. No one would think for one moment of considering Confucianism, Hinduism, or Buddhism as specially akin to Christianity, whereas Islam has been treated by some historians of the Christian

Church as belonging to the heretical offspring of the Christian religion. In fact, if we are able to abstract ourselves for a moment from all dogmatic prejudice and to become a Meccan with the Meccans, one of the "neighbours of Allah," as they call themselves, we feel in their temple, the Haram, as if we were conversing with our ancestors of five or six centuries ago. Here scholasticism with a rabbinical tint forms the great attraction to the minds of thousands of intellectually highly gifted men of all ages.

The most important lectures are delivered during the forenoon and in the evening. A walk, at one of those hours, through the square and under the colonnades of the mosque, with ears opened to all sides, will enable you to get a general idea of the objects of mental exercise of this international assembly. Here you may find a sheikh of pure Arab descent explaining to his audience, composed of white Syrians or Circassians, of brown and yellow Abyssinians and Egyptians, of negroes, Chinese, and Malays, the probable and improbable legal consequences of marriage contracts, not excepting those between men and genii; there a negro scholar is explaining the ontological evidence of the existence of a Creator and the logical necessity of His having twenty qualities, inseparable from, but not identical with, His essence; in the midst of another circle a learned *mufti* of indeterminably mixed extraction demonstrates to his pupils from the standard work of al-Ghazali the absolute vanity of law and doctrine to those whose hearts are not purified from every attachment to the world. Most of the branches of Mohammedan learning are represented within the walls of this temple by more or less famous scholars; and still there are a great number of private lectures delivered at home by professors who do not like to be disturbed by the unavoidable noise in the mosque, which during the whole day serves as a meeting place for friends or business men, as an exercise hall for Qoran reciters, and even as a passage for people going from one part of the town to the other.

In order to complete your mediaeval dream with a scene from daily life, you have only to leave the mosque by the Bab Dereybah, one of its twenty-two gates, where you may see human merchandise exhibited for sale by the slave-brokers, and then to have a glance, outside the wall, at a camel caravan, bringing firewood and vegetables into the town, led by Beduins whose outward appearance has as little changed as their minds since the day when Mohammed began here to preach the

Word of Allah.

To the greater part of the world represented by this international exhibition of Islam, as a modern Musulman writer calls it, our modern world, with all its problems, its emotions, its learning and science, hardly exists. On the other hand, the average modern man does not understand much more of the mental life of the two hundred millions to whom the barren Mecca has become the great centre. In former days, other centres were much more important, although Mecca has always been the goal of pilgrimage and the cherished abode of many learned men. Many capitals of Islam offered the students an easier life and better accommodations for their studies; while in Mecca four months of the year are devoted to the foreign guests of Allah, by attending to whose various needs all Meccans gain their livelihood. For centuries Cairo has stood unrivalled as a seat of Mohammedan learning of every kind; and even now the Uaram of Mecca is not to be compared to the Azhar-mosque as regards the number and the fame of its professors and the variety of branches cultivated.

In the last half-century, however, the ancient repute of the Egyptian metropolis has suffered a good deal from the enormous increase of European influence in the land of the Pharaohs; the effects of which have made themselves felt even in the Azhar. Modern programs and methods of instruction have been adopted; and, what is still worse, modernism itself, favoured by the late Mufti Muhammed Abduh, has made its entrance into the sacred lecture-halls, which until a few years ago seemed inaccessible to the slightest deviation from the decrees of the Infallible Agreement of the Community. Strenuous efforts have been made by eminent scholars to liberate Islam from the chains of the authority of the past ages on the basis of independent interpretation of the Qoran; not in the way of the Wahhabi reformers, who tried a century before to restore the institutions of Mohammed's time in their original purity, but on the contrary with the object of adapting Islam by all means in their power to the requirements of modern life.

Official protection of the bold innovators prevented their conservative opponents from casting them out of the Azhar, but the assent to their doctrines was more enthusiastic outside its walls than inside. The ever more numerous adherents of modern thought in Egypt do not generally proceed from the ranks of the Azhar students, nor do they generally care very much in their later life for reforming the methods prevailing there, although they may be inclined to applaud the efforts of the modernists. To the intellectuals of the higher classes the Azhar has ceased to offer great attraction; if it were not for the important funds (*waqf*) for the benefit of professors and students, the numbers of both classes would have diminished much more than is already the case, and the faithful cultivators of mediaeval Mohammedan science would prefer to live in Mecca, free from Western influence and control. Even as it is, the predilection of foreign students of law and theology is turning more and more towards Mecca.

As one of the numerous interesting specimens of the mental development effected in Egypt in the last years, I may mention a book that appeared in Cairo two years ago[20], containing a description of the present Khedive's pilgrimage to Mecca and Medina, performed two years before. The author evidently possesses a good deal of the scholastic learning to be gathered in the Azhar and no European erudition in the stricter sense of the word. In an introductory chapter he gives a summary of the geography and history of the Arabian peninsula, describes the Hijaz in a more detailed manner, and in his very elaborate account of the journey, on which he accompanied his princely master, the topography of the holy cities, the peculiarities of their inhabitants and of the foreign visitors, the political institutions, and the social conditions are treated almost as fully and accurately as we could desire from the hand of the most accomplished European scholar. The work is illustrated by good maps and plans and by a great number of excellent photographs expressly taken for this purpose by the Khedive's order. The author intersperses his account with many witty remarks as well as serious reflections on religious and political topics, thus making it very readable to those of us who are familiar with the Arabic language. He adorns his description of the holy places and of the pilgrimage-rites with the unctuous phrases used in handbooks for the hajji, and he does not disturb the mind of the pious reader by any historical criticism of the traditions connected with the House of Allah, the Black Stone, and the other sanctuaries, but he loses no opportunity to show his dislike of all superstition; sometimes, as if to prevent Western readers from indulging in mockery, he compares Meccan rites or customs with superstitious practices current amongst Jews or Christians of today.

---

20 Ar-rihlah al-Hijaziyyah, by Muhammed Labib al-Batanunf, 2d edition, Cairo, 1329 Hijrah.

This book, at whose contents many a Meccan scholar of the old style will shake his head and exclaim: "We seek refuge near Allah from Satan, the cursed!" has been adopted by the Egyptian Department of Public Instruction as a reading-book for the schools.

What surprised me more than anything else was the author's quoting as his predecessors in the description of Mecca and Medina, Burckhardt, Burton, and myself, and his sending me, although personally unacquainted with him, a presentation copy with a flattering dedication. This author and his book would have been impossible in the Moslim world not more than thirty years ago. In Egypt such a man is nowadays already considered as one of those more conservative moderns, who prefer the rationalistic explanation of the Azhar lore to putting it aside altogether. Within the Azhar, his book is sure to meet with hearty approval from the followers of Muhammed Abduh, but not less hearty disapproval from the opponents of modernism who make up the majority of the professors as well as of the students.

In these very last years a new progress of modern thought has manifested itself in Cairo in the foundation, under the auspices of Fu'ad Pasha, an uncle of the present Khedive, of the Egyptian University. Cairo has had for a long time its schools of medicine and law, which could be turned easily into university faculties; therefore, the founders of the university thought it urgent to establish a faculty of arts, and, if this proved a success, to add a faculty of science. In the meantime, gifted young men were granted subsidies to learn at European universities what they needed to know to be the professors of a coming generation, and, for the present, Christian as well as Mohammedan natives of Egypt and European scholars living in the country were appointed as lecturers; professors being borrowed from the universities of Europe to deliver lectures in Arabic on different subjects chosen more or less at random before an audience little prepared to digest the lessons offered to them.

The rather hasty start and the lack of a well-defined scheme have made the Egyptian University a subject of severe criticism. Nevertheless, its foundation is an unmistakable expression of the desire of intellectual Egypt to translate modern thought into its own language, to adapt modern higher instruction to its own needs. This same aim is pursued in a perhaps more efficacious manner by the hundreds of Egyptian students of law, science, and medicine at French, English, and some other European universities. The Turks could not freely follow such examples before the revolution of 1908; but they have shown since that time that their abstention was not voluntary. England, France, Holland, and other countries governing Mohammedan populations are all endeavouring to find the right way to incorporate their Mohammedan subjects into their own civilization. Fully recognizing that it was the material covetousness of past generations that submitted those nations to their rule, the so-called colonial powers consider it their duty now to secure for them in international intercourse the place which their natural talent enables them to occupy. The question whether it is better simply to leave the Moslims to Islam as it was for centuries is no longer an object of serious discussion, the reforming process being at work everywhere—in some parts with surprising rapidity. We can only try to prognosticate the solution which the near future reserves for the problem, how the Moslim world is to be associated with modern thought.

In this problem the whole civilized world and the whole world of Islam are concerned. The ethnic difference between Indians, North-Africans, Malays, etc., may necessitate a difference of method in detail; the Islam problem lies at the basis of the question for all of them. On the other hand, the future development of Islam does not only interest countries with Mohammedan dominions, it claims as well the attention of all the nations partaking in the international exchange of material and spiritual goods. This would be more generally recognized if some knowledge of Islam were more widely spread amongst ourselves; if it were better realized that Islam is next akin to Christianity.

It is the Christian mission that shows the deepest consciousness of this state of things, and the greatest activity in promoting an association of Mohammedan thought with that of Western nations. The solid mass of experience due to the efforts of numerous missionaries is not of an encouraging nature. There is no reasonable hope of the conversion of important numbers of Mohammedans to any Christian denomination. Broad-minded missionary societies have therefore given up the old fruitless proselytizing methods and have turned to social improvement in the way of education, medical treatment, and the like. It cannot be denied, that what they want above all to bring to Mohammedans is just what these most energetically decline to accept. On the other hand the advocates of a purely civilizing mission are bound to acknowledge that, but for rare exceptions, the desire of incorporating Mohammedan nations into our world of thought does not rouse the devoted, self-denying enthusiasm inspired by the vocation of propagating a religious belief. The ardour displayed by some missionaries in establishing in the Dar al-Islam Christian centres from which they distribute to the Mohammedans those elements of our civilization which are acceptable to them deserves cordial praise; the more so because they themselves entertain but little hope of attaining their ultimate aim of conversion. Mohammedans who take any interest in Christianity are taught by their own teachers that the revelation of Jesus, after having suffered serious corruption by the Christians themselves, has been purified and restored to its original simplicity by Mohammed, and are therefore inaccessible to missionary arguments; nay, amongst uncivilized pagans the lay mission of Islam is the most formidable competitor of clerical propagation of the Christian faith.

People who take no active part in missionary work are not competent to dissuade Christian missionaries from continuing their seemingly hopeless labour among Mohammedans, nor to prescribe to them the methods they are to adopt; their full autonomy is to be respected. But all agree that Mohammedans, disinclined as they are to reject their own traditions of thirteen centuries and to adopt a new religious faith, become ever better disposed to associate their intellectual, social, and political life with that of the modern world. Here lies the starting point for two divisions of mankind which for centuries have lived their own lives separately in mutual misunderstanding, from which to pursue their way arm in arm to the greater advantage of both. We must leave it to the Mohammedans themselves to reconcile the new ideas which they want with the old ones with which they cannot dispense; but we can help them in adapting their educational system to modern requirements and give them a good example by rejecting the detestable identification of power and right in politics which lies at the basis of their own canonical law on holy war as well as at the basis of the political practice of modern Western states. This is a work in which we all may collaborate, whatever our own religious conviction may be. The principal condition for a fruitful friendly intercourse of this kind is that we make the Moslim world an object of continual serious investigation in our intellectual centres.

Having spent a good deal of my life in seeking for the right method of associating with modern thought the thirty-five millions of Mohammedans whom history has placed under the guardianship of my own country, I could not help drawing some practical conclusions from the lessons of history which I have tried to reduce to their most abridged form. There is no lack of pessimists, whose wisdom has found its poetic form in the words of Kipling:

> *East is East and West is West,*
> *And never the twain shall meet.*

To me, with regard to the Moslim world, these words seem almost a blasphemy. The experience acquired by adapting myself to the peculiarities of Mohammedans, and by daily conversation with them for about twenty years, has impressed me with the firm conviction that between Islam and the modern world an understanding *is* to be attained, and that no period has offered a better chance of furthering it than the time in which we are living. To Kipling's poetical despair I think we have a right to prefer the words of a broad-minded modern Hindu writer: "The pity is that men, led astray by adventitious differences, miss the essential resemblances[21]."

It would be a great satisfaction to me if my lectures might cause some of my hearers to consider the problem of Islam as one of the most important of our time, and its solution worthy of their interest and of a claim on their exertion.

---

21 S.M. Mitra, Anglo-Indian Studies, London, Longmans, Green & Co., 1913, P. 232.

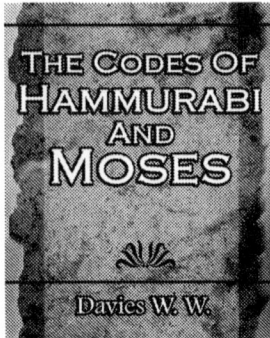

The Codes Of Hammurabi And Moses
W. W. Davies

QTY

The discovery of the Hammurabi Code is one of the greatest achievements of archaeology, and is of paramount interest, not only to the student of the Bible, but also to all those interested in ancient history...

Religion   **ISBN:** *1-59462-338-4*   **Pages:132**
MSRP $12.95

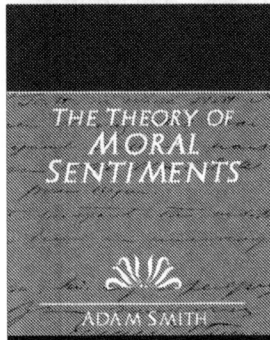

The Theory of Moral Sentiments
Adam Smith

QTY

This work from 1749. contains original theories of conscience amd moral judgment and it is the foundation for systemof morals.

Philosophy   ISBN: *1-59462-777-0*   **Pages:536**
MSRP $19.95

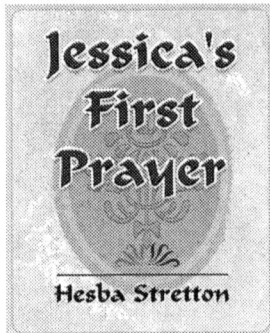

Jessica's First Prayer
Hesba Stretton

QTY

In a screened and secluded corner of one of the many railway-bridges which span the streets of London there could be seen a few years ago, from five o'clock every morning until half past eight, a tidily set-out coffee-stall, consisting of a trestle and board, upon which stood two large tin cans, with a small fire of charcoal burning under each so as to keep the coffee boiling during the early hours of the morning when the work-people were thronging into the city on their way to their daily toil...

Pages:84

Childrens   ISBN: *1-59462-373-2*   *MSRP $9.95*

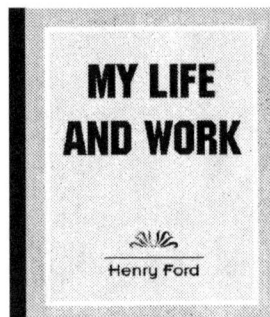

My Life and Work
Henry Ford

QTY

Henry Ford revolutionized the world with his implementation of mass production for the Model T automobile. Gain valuable business insight into his life and work with his own auto-biography... "We have only started on our development of our country we have not as yet, with all our talk of wonderful progress, done more than scratch the surface. The progress has been wonderful enough but..."

Pages:300

Biographies/   ISBN: *1-59462-198-5*   *MSRP $21.95*

www.bookjungle.com *email: sales@bookjungle.com fax: 630-214-0564 mail: Book Jungle PO Box 2226 Champaign, IL 61825*

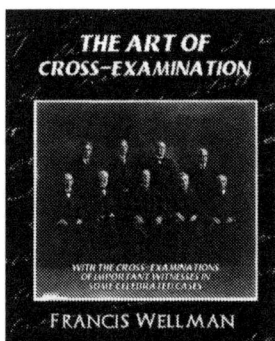

The Art of Cross-Examination
Francis Wellman

QTY

I presume it is the experience of every author, after his first book is published upon an important subject, to be almost overwhelmed with a wealth of ideas and illustrations which could readily have been included in his book, and which to his own mind, at least, seem to make a second edition inevitable. Such certainly was the case with me; and when the first edition had reached its sixth impression in five months, I rejoiced to learn that it seemed to my publishers that the book had met with a sufficiently favorable reception to justify a second and considerably enlarged edition. ..

Pages:412

Reference   **ISBN: *1-59462-647-2***   *MSRP $19.95*

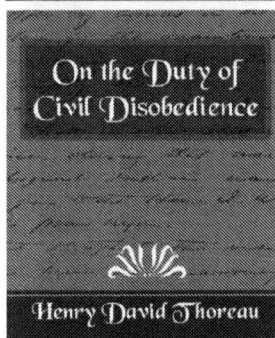

On the Duty of Civil Disobedience
Henry David Thoreau

QTY

Thoreau wrote his famous essay, On the Duty of Civil Disobedience, as a protest against an unjust but popular war and the immoral but popular institution of slave-owning. He did more than write—he declined to pay his taxes,   and was hauled off to gaol in consequence. Who can say how much this refusal of his hastened the end of the war and of slavery ?

Law   **ISBN: *1-59462-747-9***   **Pages:48**

MSRP $7.45

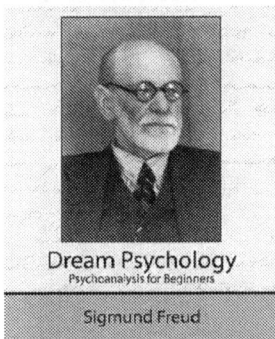

Dream Psychology Psychoanalysis for Beginners
Sigmund Freud

QTY

Sigmund Freud, born Sigismund Schlomo Freud (May 6, 1856 - September 23, 1939), was a Jewish-Austrian neurologist and psychiatrist who co-founded the psychoanalytic school of psychology. Freud is best known for his theories of the unconscious mind, especially involving the mechanism of repression; his redefinition of sexual desire as mobile and directed towards a wide variety of objects; and his therapeutic techniques, especially his understanding of transference in the therapeutic relationship and the presumed value of dreams as sources of insight into unconscious desires.

Pages:196

Psychology   **ISBN: *1-59462-905-6***   *MSRP $15.45*

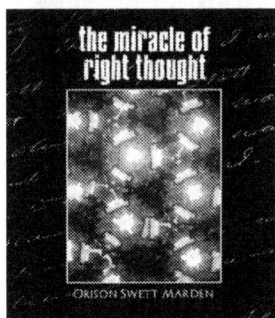

The Miracle of Right Thought
Orison Swett Marden

QTY

Believe with all of your heart that you will do what you were made to do. When the mind has once formed the habit of holding cheerful, happy, prosperous pictures, it will not be easy to form the opposite habit. It does not matter how improbable or how far away this realization may see, or how dark the prospects may be, if we visualize them as best we can, as vividly as possible, hold tenaciously to them and vigorously struggle to attain them, they will gradually become actualized, realized in the life. But a desire, a longing without endeavor, a yearning abandoned or held indifferently will vanish without realization.

Pages:360

Self Help   **ISBN: *1-59462-644-8***   *MSRP $25.45* www.bookjungle.com *email: sales@bookjungle.com fax: 630-214-0564 mail: Book Jungle PO Box 2226 Champaign, IL 61825*

QTY

☐ **The Rosicrucian Cosmo-Conception Mystic Christianity** *by Max Heindel*   ISBN: *1-59462-188-8*   **$38.95**
The Rosicrucian Cosmo-conception is not dogmatic, neither does it appeal to any other authority than the reason of the student. It is: not controversial, but is: sent forth in the, hope that it may help to clear...   New Age/Religion Pages 646

☐ **Abandonment To Divine Providence** *by Jean-Pierre de Caussade*   ISBN: 1-59462-228-0   **$25.95**
"The Rev. Jean Pierre de Caussade was one of the most remarkable spiritual writers of the Society of Jesus in France in the 18th Century. His death took place at Toulouse in 1751. His works have gone through many editions and have been republished...   Inspirational/Religion Pages 400

☐ **Mental Chemistry** *by Charles Haanel*   ISBN: *1-59462-192-6*   **$23.95**
Mental Chemistry allows the change of material conditions by combining and appropriately utilizing the power of the mind. Much like applied chemistry creates something new and unique out of careful combinations of chemicals the mastery of mental chemistry...   New Age Pages 354

☐ **The Letters of Robert Browning and Elizabeth Barret Barrett 1845-1846 vol II**   ISBN: 1-59462-193-4   **$35.95**
by Robert Browning and Elizabeth Barrett   Biographies Pages 596

☐ **Gleanings In Genesis (volume I)** *by Arthur W. Pink*   ISBN: *1-59462-130-6*   **$27.45**
Appropriately has Genesis been termed "the seed plot of the Bible" for in it we have, in germ form, almost all of the great doctrines which are afterwards fully developed in the books of Scripture which follow...   Religion/Inspirational Pages 420

☐ **The Master Key** *by L. W. de Laurence*   ISBN: 1-59462-001-6   **$30.95**
In no branch of human knowledge has there been a more lively increase of the spirit of research during the past few years than in the study of Psychology, Concentration and Mental Discipline. The requests for authentic lessons in Thought Control, Mental Discipline and...   New Age/Business Pages 422

☐ **The Lesser Key Of Solomon Goetia** *by L. W. de Laurence*   ISBN: *1-59462-092-X*   **$9.95**
This translation of the first book of the "Lernegton" which is now for the first time made accessible to students of Talismanic Magic was done, after careful collation and edition, from numerous Ancient Manuscripts in Hebrew, Latin, and French...   New Age/Occult Pages 92

☐ **Rubaiyat Of Omar Khayyam** *by Edward Fitzgerald*   ISBN:*1-59462-332-5*   **$13.95**
Edward Fitzgerald, whom the world has already learned, in spite of his own efforts to remain within the shadow of anonymity, to look upon as one of the rarest poets of the century, was born at Bredfield, in Suffolk, on the 31st of March, 1809. He was the third son of John Purcell...   Music Pages 172

☐ **Ancient Law** *by Henry Maine*   ISBN: *1-59462-128-4*   **$29.95**
The chief object of the following pages is to indicate some of the earliest ideas of mankind, as they are reflected in Ancient Law, and to point out the relation of those ideas to modern thought.   Religion/History Pages 452

☐ **Far-Away Stories** *by William J. Locke*   ISBN: 1-59462-129-2   **$19.45**
"Good wine needs no bush," but a collection of mixed vintages does. And this book is just such a collection. Some of the stories I do not want to remain buried for ever in the museum files of dead magazine-numbers an author's not unpardonable vanity..."   Fiction Pages 272

☐ **Life of David Crockett** *by David Crockett*   ISBN: *1-59462-250-7*   **$27.45**
"Colonel David Crockett was one of the most remarkable men of the times in which he lived. Born in humble life, but gifted with a strong will, an indomitable courage, and unremitting perseverance...   Biographies/New Age Pages 424

☐ **Lip-Reading** *by Edward Nitchie*   ISBN: 1-59462-206-X   **$25.95**
Edward B. Nitchie, founder of the New York School for the Hard of Hearing, now the Nitchie School of Lip-Reading, Inc, wrote "LIP-READING Principles and Practice". The development and perfecting of this meritorious work on lip-reading was an undertaking...   How-to Pages 400

☐ **A Handbook of Suggestive Therapeutics, Applied Hypnotism, Psychic Science**   ISBN: *1-59462-214-0*   **$24.95**
by Henry Munro   Health/New Age/Health/Self-help Pages 376

☐ **A Doll's House: and Two Other Plays** *by Henrik Ibsen*   ISBN: 1-59462-112-8   **$19.95**
Henrik Ibsen created this classic when in revolutionary 1848 Rome. Introducing some striking concepts in playwriting for the realist genre, this play has been studied the world over.   Fiction/Classics/Plays 308

☐ **The Light of Asia** *by sir Edwin Arnold*   ISBN: *1-59462-204-3*   **$13.95**
In this poetic masterpiece, Edwin Arnold describes the life and teachings of Buddha. The man who was to become known as Buddha to the world was born as Prince Gautama of India but he rejected the worldly riches and abandoned the reigns of power when...   Religion/History/Biographies Pages 170

☐ **The Complete Works of Guy de Maupassant** *by Guy de Maupassant*   ISBN: 1-59462-157-8   **$16.95**
"For days and days, nights and nights, I had dreamed of that first kiss which was to consecrate our engagement, and I knew not on what spot I should put my lips..."   Fiction/Classics Pages 240

☐ **The Art of Cross-Examination** *by Francis L. Wellman*   ISBN: *1-59462-309-0*   **$26.95**
Written by a renowned trial lawyer, Wellman imparts his experience and uses case studies to explain how to use psychology to extract desired information through questioning.   How-to/Science/Reference Pages 408

☐ **Answered or Unanswered?** *by Louisa Vaughan*   ISBN: 1-59462-248-5   **$10.95**
Miracles of Faith in China   Religion Pages 112

☐ **The Edinburgh Lectures on Mental Science (1909)** *by Thomas*   ISBN: *1-59462-008-3*   **$11.95**
This book contains the substance of a course of lectures recently given by the writer in the Queen Street Hall, Edinburgh. Its purpose is to indicate the Natural Principles governing the relation between Mental Action and Material Conditions...   New Age/Psychology Pages 148

☐ **Ayesha** *by H. Rider Haggard*   ISBN: 1-59462-301-5   **$24.95**
Verily and indeed it is the unexpected that happens! Probably if there was one person upon the earth from whom the Editor of this, and of a certain previous history, did not expect to hear again...   Classics Pages 380

☐ **Ayala's Angel** *by Anthony Trollope*   ISBN: *1-59462-352-X*   **$29.95**
The two girls were both pretty; but Lucy who was twenty-one who supposed to be simple and comparatively unattractive, whereas Ayala was credited, as her Bombwhat romantic name might show, with poetic charm and a taste for romance. Ayala when her father died was nineteen...   Fiction Pages 484

☐ **The American Commonwealth** *by James Bryce*   ISBN: 1-59462-286-8   **$34.45**
An interpretation of American democratic political theory. It examines political mechanics and society from the perspective of Scotsman James Bryce   Politics Pages 572

☐ **Stories of the Pilgrims** *by Margaret P. Pumphrey*   ISBN: *1-59462-116-0*   **$17.95**
This book explores pilgrims religious oppression in England as well as their escape to Holland and eventual crossing to America on the Mayflower, and their early days in New England...   History Pages 268

QTY

The Fasting Cure *by Sinclair Upton*   ISBN: *1-59462-222-1* **$13.95**
In the Cosmopolitan Magazine for May, 1910, and in the Contemporary Review (London) for April, 1910, I published an article dealing with my experiences in fasting. I have written a great many magazine articles, but never one which attracted so much attention... New Age/Self Help/Health Pages 164

Hebrew Astrology *by Sepharial*   ISBN: *1-59462-308-2* **$13.45**
In these days of advanced thinking it is a matter of common observation that we have left many of the old landmarks behind and that we are now pressing forward to greater heights and to a wider horizon than that which represented the mind-content of our progenitors... Astrology Pages 144

Thought Vibration or The Law of Attraction in the Thought World   ISBN: *1-59462-127-6* **$12.95**
by William Walker Atkinson   *Psychology/Religion Pages 144*

Optimism *by Helen Keller*   ISBN: *1-59462-108-X* **$15.95**
Helen Keller was blind, deaf, and mute since 19 months old, yet famously learned how to overcome these handicaps, communicate with the world, and spread her lectures promoting optimism. An inspiring read for everyone... Biographies/Inspirational Pages 84

Sara Crewe *by Frances Burnett*   ISBN: *1-59462-360-0*   **$9.45**
In the first place, Miss Minchin lived in London. Her home was a large, dull, tall one, in a large, dull square, where all the houses were alike, and all the sparrows were alike, and where all the door-knockers made the same heavy sound... Childrens/Classic Pages 88

The Autobiography of Benjamin Franklin *by Benjamin Franklin*   ISBN: *1-59462-135-7* **$24.95**
The Autobiography of Benjamin Franklin has probably been more extensively read than any other American historical work, and no other book of its kind has had such ups and downs of fortune. Franklin lived for many years in England, where he was agent... Biographies/History Pages 332

Name	
Email	
Telephone	
Address	
City, State ZIP	

☐ **Credit Card**   ☐ **Check / Money Order**

Credit Card Number	
Expiration Date	
Signature	

Please Mail to: Book Jungle
PO Box 2226
Champaign, IL 61825
or Fax to: 630-214-0564

ORDERING INFORMATION

web*: www.bookjungle.com*
email*: sales@bookjungle.com*
fax*: 630-214-0564*
mail*: Book Jungle PO Box 2226 Champaign, IL 61825*
or PayPal *to sales@bookjungle.com*

Please contact us for bulk discounts

DIRECT-ORDER TERMS

20% Discount if You Order
Two or More Books
Free Domestic Shipping!
Accepted: Master Card, Visa,
Discover, American Express

www.ingramcontent.com/pod-product-compliance
Lightning Source LLC
LaVergne TN
LVHW081325060426
835511LV00011B/1866